YOU DON'T HAVE TO ACHIEVE TO BE LOVED

Escape the Lies You've Been Sold to
Design the Life You Want

YOU DON'T HAVE TO ACHIEVE TO BE LOVED

Escape the Lies You've Been Sold to
Design the Life You Want

Becca Pearce

Niche Pressworks
Indianapolis, IN

YOU DON'T HAVE TO ACHIEVE TO BE LOVED

Some names, details, and identifying characteristics of individuals mentioned in the book have been changed to protect their privacy.

For permission to reprint portions of this content or for bulk purchases, contact Info@ExtendCoach.com

Author Photograph by: Shayna Hardy

Published by Niche Pressworks; NichePressworks.com
Indianapolis, IN

ISBN
Hardcover: 978-1-962956-68-0
Paperback: 978-1-962956-67-3
eBook: 978-1-962956-66-6

Library of Congress Cataloging-in-Publication Data on File at lccn.loc.gov

To Ed, for standing by me through this journey and giving me the space to figure out who I was yet to be.

To Elaina, so you can define your own success and live your own dreams now.

TABLE OF CONTENTS

A PROFOUND WAKE-UP CALL

I've known Becca for some time, and her story never fails to inspire me. The courage and resilience she has shown when life has knocked her down is nothing short of remarkable. In *You Don't Have to Achieve to Be Loved*, Becca shares raw, heartfelt stories that illustrate her journey toward living a life rooted in authenticity and self-love — and she invites you to do the same.

As I read her book, I realized I was in a season of discontent, though I couldn't quite put my finger on what was wrong. Midway through reading, my oldest son was unexpectedly hospitalized with congestive heart failure and pulmonary edema. His health crisis forced me to pause and reflect on my life, and I found myself turning to Becca's words for guidance. What I discovered was a hard truth — I wasn't truly living in alignment with my values. I was simply following the same script I had been handed my entire life.

Becca's book was a profound wake-up call. It helped me see how I was once again trying to meet everyone else's expectations instead of honoring my own. I was finally able to recognize that every time I do this, I lose confidence in myself and my unique contributions. Yet, I keep falling into the same pattern. Her change model helped me realize I can break that cycle once and for all.

What makes *You Don't Have to Achieve to Be Loved* so powerful is Becca's practical approach to creating lasting change. She doesn't just inspire you — she equips you. Her actionable steps force you to get clear on what you truly want and give you the courage to pursue it without guilt or hesitation.

If you've ever found yourself stuck in a cycle of people-pleasing, burnout, or feeling like you're just not enough, this book is a game-changer. Becca's words will remind you that you don't have to earn love — you're worthy of it simply because you exist. I highly recommend this book to anyone ready to break free from old patterns and start living a more authentic, joy-filled life.

— ANN-MARIE WHITNEY, ENTREPRENEUR

ARE YOU READY?

Do you ever find yourself wondering how it's possible — with everything you have accomplished — that you still don't feel completely satisfied? You may have had thoughts like:

I've achieved most of the things I wanted to achieve in my career. I've proven myself. I'm good at my job. I might even say I'm successful. I have a loving partner. I have a great family. I'm well off (at least well enough). On the outside, it looks like I have a great life. So, what's wrong? Why am I not happier?

If this is you, you're not alone, and you've come to the right place.

I'm Becca, and throughout this book, I share my story with you. I also share the realizations that changed my life and the process I use that has helped change the lives of my clients — both men and women.

I am living proof that you can be chewed up, spit out, and sucker punched, only to come out the other side stronger and happier. It's taken me several years to come to terms with the fact that my story will help others, but I know now that it has, does, and will.

This book is going to challenge everything you thought you knew about success and happiness. It will help you recognize what's important in life and change your definition of success so you can find the emotional courage to design the life you really want to live.

If you read this book and put in the work, it will help you design the life you actually want to live so you can finally find the happiness that has been eluding you.

How This Book Is Organized

There are two intertwining themes in this book. The first focuses on the **phases** people go through when they change and the emotions that go along with these phases.

Based on my work and research over the past eight years, I've defined four clear phases that people go through in times of significant change. The book is structured around these phases:

1. Unfortunate Awareness
2. Mourning the Past
3. One Foot In, One Foot Out
4. Clearly Me!

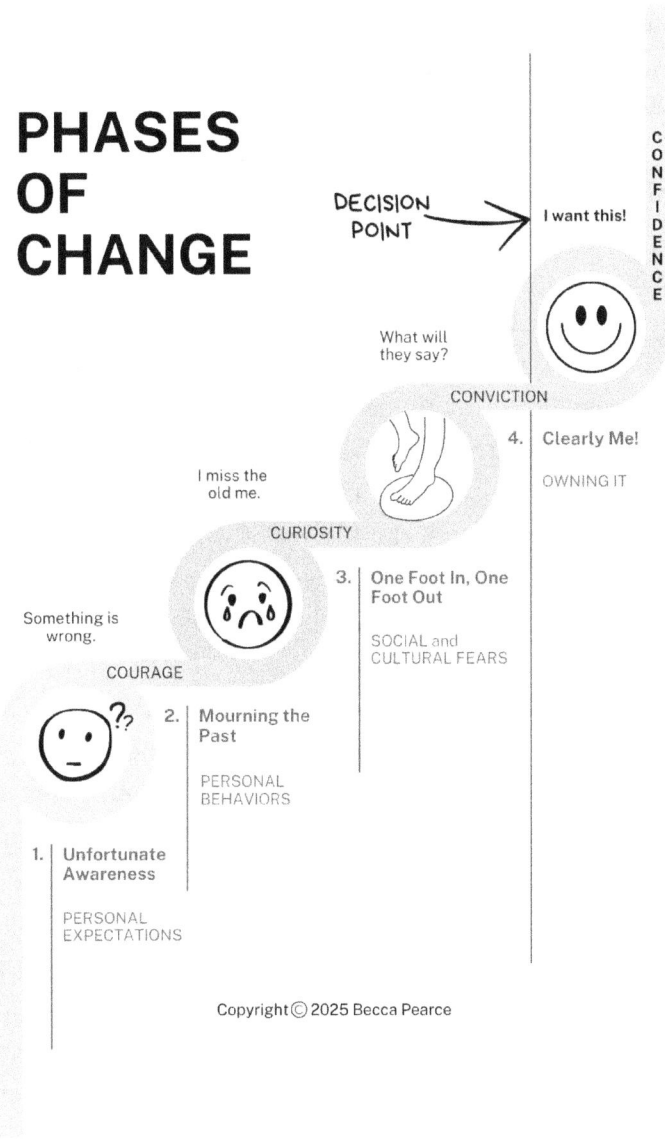

PHASES OF CHANGE

DECISION POINT

I want this!

CONFIDENCE

What will they say?

CONVICTION

4. | Clearly Me!

OWNING IT

I miss the old me.

CURIOSITY

3. | One Foot In, One Foot Out

SOCIAL and CULTURAL FEARS

Something is wrong.

COURAGE

2. | Mourning the Past

PERSONAL BEHAVIORS

1. | Unfortunate Awareness

PERSONAL EXPECTATIONS

Copyright © 2025 Becca Pearce

Each phase is characterized by specific emotions, thoughts, and fears — the questions you must come to terms with, the things that are holding you back from change, and the emotions you must tap into to move through the phase, like courage, curiosity, conviction, and confidence.

The second theme focuses on realizations that will help you move forward. Throughout the four phases, I share with you the ten **mind-blowing realizations** that allowed me to move from who I was to who I am today. These realizations are the ones that changed my life forever and are the ones that will enable you to move through each stage of change for yourself.

In fact, they are so important that you will not be able to move on *until* you work through the realization for yourself. **Rewriting your story around these realizations will change your life.**

Combined, these phases and realizations create a powerful change model that I call the Phases of Change. Everyone goes through each of these phases when implementing a change. In fact, you've likely gone through these stages before but may not have been aware of it.

It's important to note that YOUR realizations may not be exactly like mine. You may find that the general idea makes sense, but you're seeing something slightly different in yourself. That's to be expected! The book is designed to take you through your own discovery as you learn about each concept.

An important part of this process involves exploring your thoughts and feelings in writing. At the end of each chapter, you will find a **Journal Reflections** section with prompts to help you personalize and internalize each chapter's concepts.

If you journal about change, you have a greater chance of implementing it. So, find yourself a journal to keep nearby while you're reading so you can do these activities as you go through the book. They are small pieces of the full cadre of work I do with my clients. I offer them to you as a starting point on your journey toward change.

CHANGE IS HARD

Anyone who tells you change is easy either hasn't made a significant change in their lives or is lying.

BIG changes (what you do, who you are, what you relate to, who your friends are, what's important to you, how you value yourself) have lots of tentacles associated with them. These tentacles create the push and pull you will feel as you navigate the change. At times, this will likely make it harder than you'd like. The good news is that **you can do hard things**.

I wrote this book because I want YOU to be able to live the life you want without having to go through the years of pain and heartache I went through to get there. This is my gift to you.

HOW MY JOURNEY BEGAN

"You're home early," he said.

It was 10:30 p.m. I walked into my bedroom. My husband Ed was in bed reading. My six-year-old daughter Elaina was asleep in her bed, having gone yet another night without seeing her mother. It was August 2013, and as the CEO of a major state health program in Maryland, I was weeks away from launching the system that would fundamentally change the way health care was delivered for individuals and small businesses, and I was in trouble. I just didn't realize it at the time.

Two years earlier, in September 2011, I was hired as the CEO of the Maryland Health Benefit Exchange ("the Exchange"), a quasi-state agency created for the sole purpose of implementing a state-based health exchange as part of the Affordable Care Act (also known as Obamacare). When I accepted the job, the initial legislation that created the agency had been signed, but nothing else was in place. There was no legislation defining how the Exchange would work. No decisions had been made on how the technical requirements of the new systems would be achieved. There was no discussion about how the three state agencies impacted by these changes would interact with each other. And there were no plans to figure any of these things out.

I had no staff and no office, and the IT solution for implementation had not yet been decided upon. Still, getting the Exchange up and running was the most important thing on the agenda for the Governor and Lieutenant Governor — both of whom were hoping to ride the success of the Exchange into their next roles. I knew all of this going in — or so I thought. In reality, I had no idea what I was really walking into.

I was thirty-nine years old. I had a four-year-old daughter and a husband, both of whom I loved deeply. I had spent a good part of the previous few years working for Kaiser Permanente, which meant a lot of traveling to and from California. I wanted a job in Maryland. I wanted to spend more time with my family. I also wanted to follow my career trajectory right to the top.

Like a moth to a flame, I jumped at the chance to implement Obamacare. I wanted this position with every fiber of my being. I could not have believed more in what we were doing. I could not have tried harder to make it work. I could not have given more of myself (or my family) in the process.

By the time open enrollment closed in 2013, Maryland had enrolled over 300,000 previously uninsured residents in health insurance plans. The legislation written in 2012 ensured the

Exchange offered plans from the biggest insurers, and we had created a path for all three state agencies to get along. However, when the system didn't "turn on" the way it was supposed to on October 1, 2013, none of those successes mattered; the implementation was seen as a failure.

How I Defined Myself

"This is the hardest call I'll ever have to make," the Governor's chief of staff said to me when I answered the phone. It was 3:00 p.m. on December 6, 2013.

"There's going to be a newspaper article about you tomorrow morning, and we strongly suggest that to protect you and your family, you resign your position as CEO of the Exchange immediately." To be clear, he couldn't tell me to resign. He was just strongly suggesting it to protect me and my family.

Right.

I knew what I had to do. I knew I had no choice. But I refused to let go. There was so much left to do and so many people who needed me. I resolutely stayed at my desk, meeting with my team, wrapping up loose ends, and encouraging them to keep going. My biggest fear was that my team would think I had given up. I *hadn't* given up! I *don't* give up! That's not who I am! I still believed! I still wanted to see this through!

But there it was, with my signature in black and white — my resignation letter, effective immediately.

At 10:00 p.m. that night, my husband called me at the office. "Bec, come home. They fired you. It's time to leave."

Wait. What? I'm not the CEO of the Exchange anymore? What do you mean? My brain was not computing.

Without realizing it, the Exchange had become my identity. For two years, I had lived, breathed, eaten, and slept the Exchange. What would I do if I wasn't that?

Ed was relieved. When I called him after the phone call with the chief of staff, his response was, "Good."

Elaina was ecstatic. When I told her Mommy had left her job, she jumped up and down on the couch, screaming with joy.

I was hurt, confused, angry, sad, disappointed, embarrassed, and ashamed.

Amazingly, I had three lucrative job offers within three weeks. As it turns out, other people — industry people, smart people — knew it wasn't my fault. They saw through the charade. They saw strength, perseverance, expertise, and leadership. I saw a shell of myself, completely unable to see what they saw.

I turned down all three of those job offers for multiple reasons — too far away, too much time needed, or not the right fit. They were all excuses.

In reality, I was bone tired. I had nothing left. And I was still too embarrassed to function. I was sure everyone knew I had gotten fired, that everyone was looking at me differently, thinking I was incapable as a leader or pitying me for the public humiliation. I could barely leave my house.

My defense mechanism is movement. That December, I did things I'd never had time for before and things that would keep my mind and body occupied so I could avoid my feelings. One day, I spontaneously took my daughter to New York City. I watched all the kids whose moms needed coverage while schools were closed. I hosted my extended family's Christmas gathering. I cleaned out every drawer in my house.

That January, though, came a time of unspeakable sadness. I sat for days in a dark room, pondering what I had done wrong and how this could have happened. I was unable to see the great-ness others saw, forgetting that my family loved me regardless of what happened. I spent days brooding over the unfairness of it all, wallowing in my anger for everything related to Maryland government, mourning what I mistakenly thought was a friend-ship with my board chair, shocked by the actions that had taken place — and ashamed of who I was.

Learning to Be Me Again

"What are you doing right now? I'm on my way over." It was Mark, one of my dearest friends. He and I had always had this inexplicable connection. Maybe it was because we rose together in our careers; maybe it was because we understood the need to be successful. Or maybe it was because he and his wife were as close to family as you can get without being family. Whatever the reason, he was the one to pick me up, dust me off, and begin to bring me back to life.

Mark owned a Medicaid company, and he had a position for me on his leadership team. This job was right. It was in Baltimore with a friend who supported me in a market I under-stood. I jumped at the chance to start over. Interestingly, in ret-rospect, I realize he didn't really have a position for me at all; he had created it to give me the space to get back on my feet. (May we all have a friend like that when we need it most.)

While I was there, I learned how to be me again. I slowed down — made time for Ed and Elaina, called friends I hadn't had time for in years, smiled (!), and enjoyed life again. I laid to rest the identity that I had been tied to and welcomed a new-er, softer, and gentler version of myself. I was still driven, still believed achievement led to happiness, and still cared about titles and the mantra of bigger, better, faster, more. But I was becoming a more balanced version of my former self. Things were going to be okay.

You Know That's Not Normal, Right?

"Psst," she said softly.

"Honey, you know you can't talk into mommy's bad ear; you know you have to talk into mommy's good ear."

This had been going on for months. Elaina would whisper into my left ear, then run around to my right ear to say it all over again. It was a funny joke between us. But in reality, it was a warning sign I was actively choosing to ignore.

"You know that's not normal, right?"

I was at the beach with my longtime CareFirst friends — Ranaye, Cindy, Lindsey, and Jamie. Ranaye, whose words often come out of her mouth before she thinks about them (and who ends up saying some very sage things because of it), looked at me sideways.

"Single-sided deafness isn't normal," she said. "You should really get that checked out."

And so, after several years of losing hearing in my left ear, I finally acquiesced and went in for a hearing exam.

"What you're looking at is the graph of your hearing. You can see that you have lost the ability to hear all upper-range sounds in your left ear. This can sometimes be caused by a brain tumor. I'm going to send you for an MRI of your brain."

I'm sorry, what?? Did you just say you think I might have a brain tumor?

On April 14, 2015, I walked away from my MRI with a CD of my brain scan. What the tech said when she handed it to me was, "You're going to want to call your doctor." What I heard was, "You're going to die."

It was 11:00 a.m. when I got home after the MRI, and I immediately took the CD out of its sleeve and put it into my computer. (It was 2015; there were still computers with CD drives.)

I had no idea what I was going to see. I mean, who has seen an MRI of their brain before? But there, staring at me dead in the eye, was a ping-pong-ball-sized white blob in the middle of my brain scan. Anyone looking at it would know it didn't belong. Anyone would realize something was very wrong. I sat there, stunned, barely breathing, scrolling up and down, again and again, to see if anything changed. It didn't. Once my brain processed this, I simply stood up, went upstairs, and changed my clothes to go for a run.

Running For My Life

I started running when I was twenty-six years old after my boyfriend broke up with me, and I didn't know what to do with myself. From that point on, running became my therapy. As an introvert, thoughts get stuck in my brain, and the only way to work through them is to run — to let my body and legs take me away and to give my thoughts space to breathe. I run to avoid pain. I run to address pain. I run to find joy. I run to find myself.

On the day I saw the scan, I ran for my life. I didn't call Ed. I didn't even turn off my computer. Instead, I simply got up, went upstairs, changed my clothes, and literally ran out the door. I ran eight miles — crying the entire time. I ran and ran and ran until I couldn't run anymore.

I thought about what Ed and Elaina would do after I was gone and what I could do to ease the pain for them. I wondered what the dying process would look like and if I would end up in the hospice I was running past right then.

I thought about what I wanted to be remembered for and who would come to my funeral. I thought about what I should have done differently with my life. I thought about all the places I would never see and the friends I would leave behind.

I thought about my mom having to bury her daughter. I thought about the fact that I was only forty-three, and this wasn't how it was supposed to go. I thought about how much time and energy I put into being healthy and how this didn't make any sense.

I thought about Elaina, Elaina, Elaina, and Ed, Ed, Ed. I cried so hard that I had to stop running at times, bent over, gasping for air, and crying out loud.

And then... I came home, changed my clothes, and went to work.

Yes, you read that right. I went to work. Why? Because I had a 2:00 p.m. meeting that was "really important."

You see, at that point, I believed achievement, getting things done, and delivering equated to love and worthiness. I believed that this was what I had to offer the world. At one point during my run, when I thought about what I wanted to be remembered for, I thought, "I don't care if people liked me; I want to be remembered for getting shit done." My achievement drive was strong, and ignoring emotions was my modus operandi. So, going to work put me in a safe space.

I can't even remember what the "really important" meeting was about or if it made any difference if I was there. I heard nothing other than Charlie Brown voices echoing around me. I stared off into space, losing track of everything going on around me.

All I could think was, "I'm going to die." But then those thoughts would turn into thoughts about my family. And when the tears welled up in my eyes, I blinked them back and refocused on the meeting.

I'm not sure I was fooling anyone, though. At one point that day, Mark looked at me and said, "What's up with you?" I think I came back with something like, "I don't know; I guess I'm just tired." In reality, I was confused, scared, devastated about leaving my family, worried about their future, and facing my biggest fear in life — dying before Elaina could really remember me. I was not focused on work at all. I was physically and emotionally exhausted and trying to ignore all those feelings that were pushing their way to the surface.

Thankfully, I had friends in the right places, and I was able to get in to see several doctors the following week. That week, amidst the flurry of phone calls and physicians' appointments, I continued to ignore my emotions and focused only on the action steps in front of me. This is the way I chose to survive back then.

Nine days later, I was officially diagnosed with a "giant" (clinical term) vestibular schwannoma, which, because I had ignored the warning signs for so long, was growing into my brain stem. The doctors were surprised my face hadn't already been impacted, as the tumor had wrapped itself around and grown through my facial nerve. My hearing loss was the result of the tumor growing into my ear canal. I was told I needed surgery *soon* to keep it from impacting my brain stem further.

The day I was diagnosed was the day before Elaina's eighth birthday. As we were blowing out the candles on the cake, I wondered if it would be the last birthday I would ever celebrate with her.

Unfortunate Awareness

Something is
wrong.

COURAGE

1. | Unfortunate
Awareness

PERSONAL
EXPECTATIONS

UNFORTUNATE AWARENESS

When most people come to me for coaching, it's because they've come to the realization that something is off in their life or career. They may not know exactly what that something is, but they know something isn't working, and they want to work with a coach to help them fix it.

Interestingly, the reasons most people think they need coaching usually aren't the things that actually need to be addressed. For example, many people think they have problems with time management when, in reality, they have issues with boundaries, saying no, and speaking up for themselves.

Regardless of your reason, when you get to the point where you realize something isn't working for you, you have entered the Unfortunate Awareness phase of the change journey.

What You May Be Feeling

Maybe you don't want to be doing what you're doing for a living or find that you no longer have the things in common with your friends or spouse that you used to. Perhaps you know you want to retire but aren't sure who you want to be in retirement, or you can't figure out why you're antsy and generally unhappy with your life. Or maybe you've been moving through life doing things because it's what you thought you were supposed to be doing, but now you wonder what it's all for.

This phase is usually characterized by a sense of general dissatisfaction, mild to significant unease, and/or a clear understanding of a specific thing that needs to be changed. Once you recognize these feelings, you can't "unrecognize" that you're unhappy, discontent, or disappointed. You can't "unwish" for things to change. You can't "unknow" that there is a better life out there. But you *can* unlearn the things that are keeping you stuck where you are.

In the Unfortunate Awareness part of the journey, you take a hard look at your life and reflect on your personal expectations, perceptions, and beliefs. You'll evaluate long-held beliefs that have shaped your life for years. You'll start to notice, question, and eventually decide which beliefs you want to keep and which you want to modify. You'll begin to understand that there is life beyond these beliefs.

Moving through the Unfortunate Awareness phase takes courage. You have to look yourself in the mirror, question what you know and believe, and then accept that some of it may not fit anymore.

Realizations

Based on my personal and professional experience, the realizations in this section are mind-blowing. They will have you questioning everything you've known. Take the opportunity to delve deep into these realizations and use them to help you understand the water you've been swimming in. You may discover hidden expectations you've been putting on yourself or decide to take a closer look at things you've inadvertently been believing to be true in life.

Until you come to terms with these realizations, they will continue to hold you where you are now.

The realizations in this phase are:

- You Don't Have to Achieve to Be Loved
- Time Is All That Matters
- Vulnerability Is THE KEY to Lasting Change

As you work through this phase, be cognizant that fear is a big part of what keeps you stuck. Fear blocks you from looking at things differently. It can keep you from trying new things, and it can prevent you from letting go of the beliefs that got you to where you are today.

Courage

This phase will require you to lean into your courage and look very closely at why you are where you are today. You will have to grapple with which behaviors you want to keep and which you want to let go of. It's only when you've made these choices about what stays and what goes that you can begin to move forward with a new vision of what your future can hold.

YOU DON'T HAVE TO ACHIEVE TO BE LOVED

Reading that title out loud makes it seem so obvious. And yet, it took a life-altering event for me to understand this was true.

When I came home from the hospital five days after my surgery, I was unable to walk, unable to go to the bathroom on my own, unable to eat solid foods, and still in an indescribable amount of pain. I threw up when I turned my head and felt like I was falling out of bed when I was lying still. To put it simply, I needed round-the-clock support for several weeks.

Ed stayed home for the first week to take care of me. My parents, who had luckily moved back to town the October before, stayed with me when Ed couldn't. They took Elaina to the bus stop and held our household together.

I slept most of that first week in the extra bedroom (well, I tried to sleep — real sleep does not come easily after head surgery). Ed would set alarms throughout the night to deliver my meds to me, and I would call for someone to help me when I had to use the bathroom. During the day, I would sit semi-upright on the couch, where I faded in and out of consciousness, just waiting for 7:00 p.m. when *Jeopardy!* would come on so I could allow myself to go back to bed when it was over.

I live in a classic suburban neighborhood (picture the fifties television show *Leave It to Beaver*). So, I shouldn't have been surprised when the neighborhood created a food train for us. Every other night for a month, someone from the street would deliver us a home-cooked dinner.

But, somehow, this simple act of community became one of the most mind-blowing moments of my recovery and changed my life forever.

When the first person came to the door, my immediate response was, "What? Why would they do that? I've never done anything to earn that." And when I found out it was the entire neighborhood doing this for us for a whole month, I was completely overwhelmed and *very* confused.

I could not stop wondering why this was happening. Why would they do this for me? I was always at work and wasn't even sure I could name everyone who was bringing food! I never had time to interact with people in my neighborhood, and when I did, I probably wasn't all that friendly. So, I really couldn't figure out why they would do this for me.

At the time, I assumed that since I hadn't achieved anything that mattered to them — especially since I had failed at the Exchange — I didn't deserve their support or love. I was still ashamed and embarrassed (a year and a half later) that I had failed. And yet, no one in the neighborhood seemed to care about it, and no one seemed to care that I hadn't had time for them in the past.

I was flabbergasted.

WHY THIS MATTERS

After coaching hundreds of successful people and talking to hundreds of others, I've come to realize I am not alone, and you are not alone. There is an entire world of people out there who tie their self-worth to their successes. They believe they are unworthy of love if they are not contributing in some significant way.

This single realization rocked the foundation of everything I had ever known and changed the way I looked at the world. It was the beginning of my journey and has been the beginning of the journey for most of my clients as well.

If you've achieved professional success, I am willing to bet you hold some form of this belief about yourself. And if you're reading this, thinking I have twelve heads, and your brain can't even compute what the sentence is saying to you — "What do you mean? Of course, I must achieve to be loved!" — you are definitely one of those people.

Are you ready to stop the cycle you're in? Are you ready to stop believing you must continue on your current path? Are you ready to stop striving for more, more, more when it doesn't make you happy?

If you're ready to move out of the Unfortunate Awareness you're experiencing now, you need to realize this: **You do NOT need to achieve to be loved. It's that simple. People love you for who you are, not for what you have achieved.**

Where Does This Come From?

To help explain how we got to this place, let me back up a second and get a bit scientific (well, my version of scientific). From the moment we are born, everything we experience in life creates a reaction in our brain. The brain is made up of about 90 billion neurons that all hold and transmit information. Information flows along neural pathways (the connections between neurons) via electrochemical signals.

Right now, think about an Oreo. Whether you love or hate them, you have a reaction. Is your mouth watering? Are you thinking of a specific kind of Oreo — maybe double stuff or dark chocolate? Is there guilt (or pleasure) associated with an Oreo? At some point in your life, a neural pathway was created that led you to feel and think whatever you just felt and thought about that Oreo.

Neural pathways are created by your experiences. Some of these experiences and pathways are more ingrained than others. My neural pathways for achievement and love were very deep. As a child, I was taught that being smart is the greatest gift. My brothers and I were praised when we achieved. But even when we did achieve, the praise was fleeting or understated. For example, when I brought home straight A's on my report card, my mother would say, "Well, we expect you to get all A's, so it's nothing to congratulate you for." So, the next time, I would try even harder to get noticed and praised.

For forty-three years, I had been chasing one simple "I'm proud of you" from my mother. Because I never got it, I tried harder and harder and did more and more in an attempt to gain it. Making CEO by the time I'm thirty-nine! How can she not be proud of that? In *Forbes Magazine* — I mean, yes! She has to be proud of that, right?!

But I never got it. I never got the elusive "I'm proud of you." And so, the cycle continued. The neural pathway became more entrenched, and I tried even harder to be someone others would marvel at. The problem was that I wasn't able to marvel at myself. I believed I was not worthy unless I achieved something amazing.

For many people I coach, when they are working through this belief, they find that their neural pathway connecting achievement to love also stems from their upbringing. They had been praised for the outcome instead of the effort.

But that's not the only place this thinking can come from.

Other Influences on Self-Worth

The way we view our own worth is complicated. As we've discussed, much of it comes from early life experiences. However, the society we live in can also be a factor. Too often, success and productivity are glorified instead of creativity or the process. The learning that can come from failing forward is undervalued.

Further, social norms and expectations can be confusing. As women, we're told we can have it all, yet we are often minimized at work for having a family. As men, you're told you must be the breadwinner, the fixer, the provider, but your family gets upset when you work late or carry the stress of the job home with you. In these examples, society defines and sets expectations for you. You try to do the right thing, but it rarely works out the way society says it should, which leaves you with a lot of contradictions and turmoil.

Today, social media is also a factor in the mix. When we compare ourselves to the way others present themselves (often exaggerated), it can, once again, reinforce a pathway where achievement translates to love and admiration.

When you're programmed to tie your worth to achievement, getting mixed messages about your success on a regular basis only creates more pressure to succeed. You think that if you just get that next title or more money, people will appreciate all your accomplishments. When that doesn't happen, you push even harder, and the pathway gets deeper.

Embracing Unfortunate Awareness

Problems arise when *not* achieving something causes you to question your self-worth. Problems also arise when you *do* achieve what you want but still aren't happy. This is how and when you end up in Unfortunate Awareness, realizing something isn't right.

I now know that my mother is, indeed, very proud of me. I don't need to hear it to know. I know she has her own limits, which were passed down to her by her parents from their generational and cultural backgrounds. And I now know that it's okay. I've now learned to believe in myself enough to see how proud my mother and father are of me. I've learned how chasing achievement is a dead-end road.

After my time at the Exchange, the proof that I didn't have to achieve to be loved was there — I just didn't recognize it. It was jokes about me being the fall guy. It was a six-year-old jumping on the couch in unbridled joy. It was Ed telling me how much he loved me. It was family telling me to let it go and move on. It was friends getting me up off the couch and believing in my abilities.

It wasn't until the doorbell rang with that first dinner — when a neighbor I didn't really know offered the kindness and support I would have never thought to give her — that I began to understand that people didn't care what my title was or whether I had done something for them. People saw a neighbor in need and stepped in.

I am now aware that this is simply called humanity. I get how this experience may be commonplace for many of you. But it blew my mind. My neural pathway was so strong that "This is normal, and you deserve this" simply did not compute.

Your realization may come from something just as simple. Or maybe you're still questioning whether I'm right.

Think about it. Do you actually care what your friends do for a living? Do you like them more when they get promoted? Do you like them less if they switch jobs or lose their job?

My guess is no.

People will forget what you said, people will forget what you did, but people will never forget how you made them feel.
— MAYA ANGELOU

WHAT YOU CAN DO

The belief that people love you because of what you've achieved is a hard one to let go of. After all, your belief in this belief may have gotten you to where you are today, right?

Wrong.

This is called a false cause fallacy and occurs when someone incorrectly assumes that one event causes another, even though there is no real connection between the two events or any evidence to support the claim.[1]

In my case, I assumed that I received love because I succeeded. In reality, I have been loved my whole life by many people. And it's not because I got an A on my report card, won a race, got promoted, or had a certain title. I may have been *noticed* or *complimented* for these things, but that was not love. People loved me regardless of whether I achieved or not.

This may sound familiar to many of my fellow overachievers.

Best Friend Language

To try to shift this way of thinking, I recommend using what I call "best friend language." Imagine a friend coming to you, upset that they didn't get promoted. Or think about your child telling you they're disappointed that they got a B on a math test.

Would you ever say, "Oh geez, well, I don't love you anymore because you didn't get your promotion." Or "Oh, honey, I only love you when you get an A." That sounds insane, right?

But that's exactly what we allow our brains to do! We allow our internal dialogue to say things to ourselves that we would never say to someone we love. And we believe it because we've believed it for years.

Recognize

Now that you've tried the best-friend-language exercise, I suspect you have a greater appreciation for the power of your brain and its internal dialogue. What I'd like you to do next is notice when your internal dialogue is saying something negative. Are you berating yourself without even realizing it? What assumptions does your internal dialog make?

When you learn to recognize that voice, you may be surprised by how often your internal dialog pressures you in a way no one else would ever do or assumes others won't love you because _____ (fill in the blank). You need to remind yourself that **this is not true**. You are loved because you are you.

Internal Validation

The sad downside of the belief that you have to achieve to be loved is that it's robbing you of joy and connectedness. It's keeping you from listening to the voice in your head that says you're tired or unhappy.

When you're bound to this belief, you believe that achieving more is the only way to finally get what you're looking for. You are forever searching for external validation that you are enough.

The hard truth is that you may never (probably won't ever) get the external approval you're looking for. And I can tell you this — if you do get it, it still won't be enough for you. The only place to find the approval you're ultimately looking for is inside yourself. Learning to find internal validation will help break this old mindset and set you on a new path.

JOURNAL REFLECTIONS

As I mentioned, my realizations may not match yours exactly. The prompts below will give you an opportunity to reflect on the content in a way that is specific to your situation. I strongly encourage you to stop reading, find your journal, and dive into your own version of this belief.

1. Fill in the blanks for this statement: I must _____ in order to _____.

   - Where does this belief come from?
   - How has this belief been fanned and/or supported over the years?
   - Is this belief true?
   - If it's not true, what could be true?

2. Where are you missing signs that people love you regardless of whether you achieve?

TIME IS ALL
THAT MATTERS

525,600 minutes
525,000 moments so dear
525,600 minutes
How do you measure, measure a year?

In daylights, in sunsets
In midnights, in cups of coffee
In inches, in miles
In laughter, in strife
In 525,600 minutes — how do you measure a year in the life?

— "SEASONS OF LOVE," *RENT*, JONATHON LARSON

It took a brain tumor for me to truly grasp how precious a gift time is. You never know exactly how much you have in your lifetime, so there's no time to waste. Now is the moment to start figuring out what you really want in life — and this realization is all about that.

It was five weeks from the day I was diagnosed to the day I was on the operating table. During that time, I would like to say I quit my job, spent every waking moment with my family, and lived every day to the fullest. But that's not what happened.

I went to work. I went to more doctor's appointments than I'd ever been to in my life. I put Elaina on the bus every day, making heart signs and blowing kisses through the window like nothing was wrong. I "kept on keeping on," trying to keep the routine that created safety and security for everyone involved, including me.

Behind the scenes, I ran. I ran in the morning. I ran at lunch. I ran after work. I tried to physically run myself into the ground, thinking that, just maybe, I would sleep that night. But, every night, like clockwork, I woke up.

My mind spun with wishes and regrets. I wished that I could turn back time — if I had gone to the doctor earlier, could I have changed the outcome? I desperately wished to be alive to watch Elaina grow up and mourned the moments I envisioned missing, like her graduation and wedding. I worried about how much time I had left to spend with the ones I loved and grieved the years I had already lost.

Every time I thought about what I would miss, it wasn't things or places. It was *time*. Time to be with Elaina as she grew up. Time to reconnect with Ed in a way we hadn't since before the Exchange. Time to share my stories and thoughts and laughter and joy. AND time to prove myself one more time.

WHY THIS MATTERS

We often pause and take a moment when someone we know dies before their time. We may even continue to think about it over the next few days, considering what we want to do differently. But those thoughts eventually disappear into the background — lost in grocery store trips, carpools, work responsibilities, and life.

But what would you do if you woke up one day and learned you didn't have any more time? The moment I got my diagnosis, I could feel time disappearing. It was terrifying how quickly time, which felt so abundant, could suddenly become so scarce. I became consumed with thoughts about time — the absence of time, how I wish I could have spent the time I already had differently, and even how I would spend my future time if I had a chance to have it.

Then, I realized with resignation and recognition that everything else in life was a complete lie. My title didn't matter! How much money I made didn't matter! *Nothing in the world mattered more than time.* It is the most real and important thing in our lives.

Understanding the value of time and its worth to you is what this realization is all about. Without stopping to identify what time means to you and how you want to spend it, there's a very good chance you will never make it out of Unfortunate Awareness. If you don't realize time is fleeting, you will continue with the thought that "one day," you will make it happen. Or you'll be happy when _____. But that "when" or "one day" may never come.

Time is scarce. It's our only nonrenewable resource, and it's the most important one you have. Every moment you use it doing something you don't value or may regret in the future is a waste of this most valuable resource.

It's only when you acknowledge the scarcity of time that the urgency to make a change outweighs the fear of making it. Understanding this scarcity allows you to envision what *could* be if you were spending your time in a way that aligns with your personal values. Accepting this scarcity allows you to take steps to make that vision a reality, propelling you out of the Unfortunate Awareness doldrums and catapulting you into action.

How Do We Spend Our Time?

There are twenty-four hours in each day. On average, we spend eight of them sleeping and eight of them working.

What do we do with the other eight hours of our day?

Let's start at the beginning of the day. If you're like many households, the morning is crammed full of frenzied exchanges: "Are you ready yet?" "Have you seen my backpack?" "Where are your shoes?" and "We have to go!" When you finally get everyone out the door and to their respective destinations for the day, we'll say an hour has passed.

Let's assume your workday ends around 5:30 p.m. (I'm feeling generous today!). Depending on the age of your kids, you might go straight to practices or maybe they will get to play with their friends. Then, it's time for homework, dinner, and the bedtime routine. If you're lucky, you've gotten your kids to bed by 9:30 p.m. So, that's another four hours of potentially harried time.

Altogether, that's five hours with the family per day (in some form). This translates to 20 percent of our weekdays spent interacting with our family.

Let that sit for a second. As working parents, we spend approximately 20 percent of our weekdays with our children. How focused are you during that time? How engaged are you with your child?

And what about your partner? How engaged are you when you are with them? Do you laugh? Do you really listen, or is your mind elsewhere? Many of the people I know either have their minds still at work or on to the next thing that needs to get done. **Take a moment and ask yourself: How present were you with your family last night?**

When I was at the Exchange, I went weeks on end without being home early enough to put my daughter to bed. I went weeks without having dinner with my husband. And even when I was home, I wasn't really home. I was thinking about a meeting, looking at emails on my phone, or answering a call from a board member.

I will never get that time back. I can never go back and watch Elaina grow over those years. I'll never have a second chance to connect with Ed in a way that pulled us together. And I can never create memories with my family from that time period. It is the single biggest regret of my life.

It's so easy to get caught up in that important meeting or how we're doing at work that we often forget that the most important job we have is to be present for the ones we love. We are not promised tomorrow. We aren't even promised our next minute. So it's time to focus on what's most important: time with your loved ones.

Another Way We're Distracted

It's no secret that cell phones have had a big impact on how we spend our valuable time. Here are a few facts that may surprise you:

- The average person spends over 4 hours on their phone each day.[2]
- If you're a social media user, you spend almost 2.5 hours a day on social media.[3]
- The average person checks/unlocks their phone 144 times a day.[4]
- We swipe, tap, or click 2,617 times a day.[5]
- 89 percent of Americans check their phone within the first 10 minutes of waking up.[6]
- 76 percent of people check work emails after work hours (on their phone).[7]

I don't need to go on. You are likely already aware that your phone is robbing you of time each day that you could be using more intentionally.

We live in an era in which we are constantly bombarded with information. Anecdotally, scientists think the average person today receives more information *each day* than the average person did *in a lifetime* in 1900! It's no wonder we are going in ten different directions at once. Distractions are constant.

And then there is email. When you check email outside of work hours, you shift your priorities away from family or friend time and hand it to someone else. In that moment, those loved ones have lost you.

You may never be able to completely limit the hours in your workday or the amount of information thrown at you. But you *can* be very clear about how you choose to spend your time and learn to set boundaries so you can get what you want out of every moment you have.

WHAT YOU CAN DO

I start every speaking engagement by asking the attendees, "Why is this seminar important to you?" because I want every person in that room to be selfish with their time. I want them to suck every tidbit out of every moment they have. I want people to realize that time is fleeting, and they don't want to look back and regret frittering it away.

I want *you* to look at everything in your life the same way. Who is important in your life? What do you really care about at the end of the day? Make a list and focus on THAT! (Seriously, stop and make a list of the important people in your life, and define what's important to you at the end of each day.) Be specific about what you want to do with your time. Be selfish about how you use it, what you say yes to, and, more importantly, what you say NO to.

There are many people who will tell you to "be present." While I fully subscribe to this as much as I can, that is not really who I am as a coach and not what I'm going to suggest.

I am pragmatic and driven, so this section focuses on actions you can take today to change the way you invest your time. Specifically, we'll discuss strategies for saying no and talk about how to be intentional with your time.

Say No!

Do you know how many of my female clients tell me they have trouble saying no? Too many to count. Want to guess how many of my male clients tell me they have trouble saying no? I can count them on one hand.

Why do people — especially women — have an aversion to this simple word? In my anecdotal research based on client interactions, it normally comes down to a few things:

1. **You're a people pleaser.** You have been taught that you should avoid conflict, keep the room stable, and keep everyone happy. Everyone but you, that is.

2. **You feel guilty.** The thought of letting someone down automatically cues feelings of guilt. For some reason, you believe that you should always be the one to have time to help others out. You put their needs above your needs.

3. **You don't want others to think badly of you.** You don't want to look like you're selfish or uncaring toward others, and you fear that others will think badly of you if you say no.

I often say, "Not saying no is a cheap way of getting others to like you." It's also the quickest way to make your life more hectic, send your stress through the roof, and end up burned out.

Catie, one of my clients, is a very accomplished CEO of a business that she grew from $3M to $12M in just five years. She has two kids in grade school and, at one point, was serving on three executive boards. But she didn't feel accomplished anywhere other than work. She didn't see her family as much as she wanted, and when she did, she was admittedly distracted. She also felt like her board work was not up to par, a bit of a waste of her time, and stressful because of the time commitments.

Catie came to one of my retreats, and as we sat on the patio having a one-on-one discussion about her realizations from the day, I looked at her and said, "You do know you don't have to achieve something to be worthy, right? And you know you only have this time with your kids once."

I felt like I could see into her head as her neurons were lighting on fire. Talk about brain exploding! She sat quietly for a minute and then said, "I'm done. I've learned everything I need to learn. I'm changing my ways right now."

Over the next twenty-four hours, she created an action plan. She set meetings on her calendar for time with her children and committed to putting her phone down during those times. She refused to take on work commitments during this time. She spoke to her leadership team about the changes she wanted to make and asked them to hold her accountable. She committed to her husband that she would be present and asked him to also hold her accountable. She quit one of her boards immediately and gave a second board notice that she would leave at the end of her term. She wanted her time to be HER TIME, focused on what she realized was really important to her. She was all in on her changes.

Now, when Catie is at work, she's at work. She has not changed her focus on the growth of her company, and she continues to be one of the strongest and most gifted leaders I have ever coached. She is still accomplished and still growing her business. The difference is that she is now also present for her kids, spending time with her husband, and finding time for herself.

She learned how to say no.

You can do it too.

Every time you say yes to something you don't want to do, you take time away from what you really *do* want to do. Saying yes to others robs you and your family of time — time you could be spending living the life you want to live. Imagine walking out of your doctor's office after finding out you only have months to live. Are you going to be happy you spent the last four Tuesday evenings working on the guest list for the Association dinner?

Now, let me be clear. I am not suggesting you say no, just to say no. What I am suggesting is that before you say no, you find the time and space to ask yourself if what's being asked of you is something you want to spend time doing. Remember: People have a right to ask you for help with something. You have just as much right to say no.

Let's talk about how you can learn to say no.

The Yes or No Process

For many people, the "Yes" reply is entrenched and reactionary. But there is a process you can go through before you commit to help, and it allows you to decide whether you want to say yes or no. The steps below outline how you can evaluate these requests.

1. A person asks you the question.
2. Stop. Do not answer the question right away!
3. Ask a few questions to gain clarity. Think about what you need to know before you say yes. What are the

expectations? What is the commitment you're agreeing to? How long will it last? Have others been asked? What happens if you say no?

4. Once you understand the commitment, think about what you would need to give up in order to confidently say yes to the request. (Note: at all times, there is at least one thing you're giving up if you say yes to something — even if it's a thirty-minute nap you have to skip to feed the neighbor's cat.) Make sure you understand what that trade-off is.

5. After you've thought about all of the above, you can then decide if this is time that you're willing to give up.

6. If it's not, that's okay! You can say no!

The Three-Step No

Put simply, "No." is a complete sentence. But for those of you who are less apt to use that word when asked to do something, I recommend the following three-step approach:

1. Thank you.
2. No, because...
3. Consider this instead...

This approach allows you to recognize the opportunity, give the person asking a clear understanding of what is more important to you right now, and then offer them support in another way.

Here's an example response: "Thank you for the opportunity and for thinking of me! I appreciate your faith in me. At this time, I need to be focused on _____." Insert what you are truly focused on in your life at the time (i.e., building my business, being with my teenagers, spending more time on me!). Then add, "So, I'm going to have to say no. I do appreciate you thinking of me! I think Jane would be a great fit for what you're looking for."

The important thing here is that they clearly hear you saying no; there is no confusion, no slippery slope, no question about your answer. They have also heard *why* you're saying no, so they don't come back and ask the same question next week. And finally, you're supporting them with an alternative solution.

How NOT to Say No

While it's important to learn the right way to say no, it is equally important to talk about how NOT to do it.

Don't ghost people. Don't assume that avoiding the conversation is good enough. Respect people enough to answer them directly. If they were brave enough to ask, you should be brave enough to respond directly.

Don't say yes and then not really show up (either literally or figuratively). This is worse than saying no at the start. People will not only lose faith in your abilities but will now be left in a worse spot than if you'd said no to begin with.

Don't just hope they can see that you don't want to do it. Don't dance around the ask and give mixed signals. You're an adult. It's up to you to own your decisions and communicate them.

Be Intentional About Your Time

We often don't realize how much time we fritter away without thinking about it. I tell my clients that if they don't know where their time is going, it's time to take a hard look at how they're spending it.

Until you take the time to understand how you're currently allocating your time and how you WANT to be spending your time, you will be stuck in the place you are today.

Time is fleeting. Time is precious. You will never get moments back. **Being intentional about your time is one of the first key steps in learning to be present in your life.**

Say no to the things that will take you away from your loved ones too often. Be intentional about your time every day so you have the energy to spend on what matters. Put down your phone. Leave your work at work. ENJOY the moments you have by focusing on the things that bring you joy because time is something we are not guaranteed.

JOURNAL REFLECTIONS

Now, it's time to focus and reflect. The questions here will help you become intentional about how you want to spend your time moving forward and what to change.

1. Where do you wish you could spend more time?

2. What have you said yes to recently that you now think you should have said no to?

3. Why did you say yes?

4. What practice do you need in order to learn how to say no comfortably?

VULNERABILITY IS THE KEY TO LASTING CHANGE

By now, you've started to recognize specific parts of your life that aren't quite how you want them to be, which puts you right in the middle of Unfortunate Awareness. While you may acknowledge that things aren't right, you're still hesitant to make a change because you're afraid to look (or be) vulnerable.

As difficult as it may seem, getting where you want to be requires vulnerability, which is likely to make you feel uncomfortable. I'm not going to tell you that it's easy, but I will tell you that to move forward, it's necessary to be vulnerable.

Being vulnerable takes courage. The good news? You can be courageous.

During the last months at the Exchange, I knew things were less than ideal. I only slept about four hours each night. I usually woke up around 2:30 a.m. and was unable to get back to sleep, thinking of all the things I needed to do. Instead of fretting, I would get out of bed, do some work until about 5 a.m., and then exercise before Elaina and Ed got up so I could spend the limited time I had with them before our collective days started.

Every morning, I dropped Elaina off at morning care right when they opened, answered a call from my board chair, and then spent the rest of the drive into the office crying on the phone with Ed. There were so many different tentacles of the implementation that needed to be addressed, so many politicians to appease, so many technical issues to fix, so much legislation to read. On top of that, I was *exhausted*. I was struggling to hold it all together.

All my stress and anxiety came out in tears on my way to work every day. But when I got to work, I would wipe the tears away, reapply my makeup, stand tall, and walk in like nothing was wrong. I had armor that was unbreakable. No one would see me sweat.

I thought I needed to have all the answers. I thought showing any "chinks in the armor" would lead others to think we were failing. I thought everyone on my team was looking to me to save the day. In reality, the people on my team wondered if I was human. They thought I was disconnected from the situation. Quite frankly, they didn't really like me.

Throughout my career, I was taught to leave emotions at the door, to laugh only with your friends (and only behind closed doors), and to never ever let them see you sweat — or, God forbid, cry. Being a strong leader meant showing up like a stereotypical businessman — emotionless, ruthless, and always focused on the prize.

So, I carried that with me to the Exchange. "Leave your emotions at the door," was my mantra, "We have sh** to do." I even carried it with me when I landed on my feet again at Mark's company. I had no room for emotion or drama at work.

But after surgery, when I returned to the office, I was changed in all ways. It was impossible to miss the impact the surgery had had on me physically. I was twenty pounds lighter, my face was paralyzed, I couldn't speak well, and I had trouble walking.

It was also impossible not to see the impact the surgery had on me emotionally. I cared more about people now. I asked how they were doing. I appreciated different opinions and believed in positive intent. I shared my own feelings and took steps to change the culture of the organization. Unfortunately, these behaviors were not necessarily true of me before.

It was my vulnerabilities and, more importantly, my ability to embrace those vulnerabilities that allowed me to become the new version of myself. Without those vulnerabilities, I would never have changed; I would have kept that armor on — possibly forever.

In October 2015, five months after my surgery and soon after I had returned to work, there was a 5K walk for the Brain Tumor Society in Baltimore. Twenty-five employees from the company showed up to walk with me — some of whom I couldn't name. But they all felt like they knew me now in a way they had never known me before.

I had become human to them.

WHY THIS MATTERS

It's simple. Until you embrace vulnerability, you cannot change.

The problem is that learning how to embrace vulnerability is not simple. As humans, we are biologically built to hide our vulnerabilities in order to stay alive. As a leader, somewhere along the line, you've learned to hide your emotions from your colleagues. You likely think this shows that you're confident and in charge. You may even be worried that showing your friends any of your true vulnerabilities will make them think about you differently.

But this armor you've built is keeping you from making the change you want to make now. It's the thing that is keeping you stuck in Unfortunate Awareness — sad that things aren't right and unable to move toward a meaningful solution because you're afraid of looking vulnerable.

Coming to terms with this vulnerability takes courage. And when you learn to embrace it, you begin to open up to change in a way that allows you to move to the next phase.

What Is Vulnerability?

Many of us have been taught that vulnerability is weakness. In fact, if you do a search of synonyms for vulnerable, you'll find a list of words that generally have negative connotations. "Weak" is right at the top, followed by words like defenseless, exposed, and unsafe. *Merriam-Webster's* definition of vulnerability reads, "capable of being physically or emotionally wounded; open to attack or damage."[8] No wonder we see it as a bad word! How could it be a good thing?

Brené Brown, author, researcher, and expert on vulnerability and shame, describes vulnerability as "having the courage to show up and be seen when we have no control over the outcome."[9] She explains that it's also the birthplace of innovation, creativity, and change.

Vulnerability Makes You More Likable

Think of the most invulnerable person you know. Get them in your mind. Do you like them? Do you trust them? Do you want to be their friend? Do you feel like you know them? My guess is no to all of the above questions.

Now, think of the most welcoming person you know or a person you trust. Why do you find them welcoming? Why do you trust them? I'm guessing it's because they've shared aspects of themselves with you. They've been just vulnerable enough for you to feel safe with them.

There's a misconception we've been sold that people like you more if you're strong. In reality, people tend to like others who are open and honest enough to share their feelings. Being honest enough to share your feelings makes you more relatable and authentic. Opening up makes others comfortable opening up to you, and this honesty creates mutual respect. It can also be scary.

Opening up and being vulnerable takes courage because, by definition, you are opening yourself up to an unknown response from the other person, and that can feel unsafe. Interestingly, the converse is true: sharing pieces of yourself creates a safe environment. It lowers the defenses of the other party and encourages them to share more as well. It demonstrates your trust in that person and helps strip away the barriers you may have put in place.

When you are vulnerable, it is a signal that you value the relationship enough to show up honestly. A good example of this is when you enter into a new romantic relationship. It's not until you let your defenses down and open yourself up to the potential of being hurt that you find the space to truly love the other person and to let them love you.

> **Reflection:** What if you found the courage to be vulnerable (or more vulnerable) in all your relationships — with friends, colleagues, sisters, brothers, and neighbors? Compare that to how you relate to them now. What barriers do you have in place? How might sharing just one piece of yourself in a new way change that relationship?

Vulnerability Makes You a Stronger Leader

Let's go back to Brené Brown's definition of vulnerability and apply it to the work setting. *Vulnerability is having the courage to show up when you can't control the outcome.* What is more vulnerable than showing up to a meeting when you don't have the answer? How many times have you stayed up late or crammed to get something done just so you could show up to the meeting with an answer? Meanwhile, there are ten people in the room who all have ideas that might make the answer better, stronger, or more innovative. But since you had to prove that you had the answer, you've squashed not only innovation but the ability of your team to show up and think bigger. And you also come across as a know-it-all.

I developed the "How Vulnerability Makes You a Stronger Leader" chart to explain how you may inadvertently be putting yourself in the wrong quadrant as a leader. As you look at this, see if you can see where you would land and where you would put other people you know.

Someone with high vulnerability and low strength is meek, weak, and helpless. Someone with low vulnerability but low strength is usually a jerk and also ineffective.

If you add strength to the mix, you begin to describe people you think of as leaders. Someone with high strength and low vulnerability tends to appear to have all the answers. They seem untouchable and unflappable but also uninspiring for most people around them.

When you have strength and add a bit of vulnerability — for example, asking for thoughts on something you don't have the answer to or admitting you made a mistake or laughing because you overslept this morning — you become authentic, courageous, and trustworthy. This is the leader people will follow to the ends of the earth.

Which leader do you want to be?

HOW VULNERABILITY MAKES YOU A STRONGER LEADER

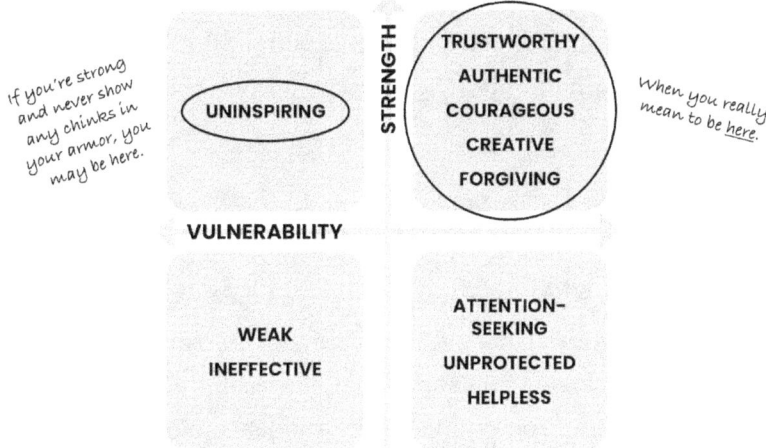

Vulnerability Is THE KEY To Lasting Change

By definition, change involves doing something new. Doing something new means you haven't mastered it, don't know how it will turn out, and may make a mistake. Change is scary, and it requires courage to move forward.

If you have spent your life trying not to show your vulnerabilities, you have probably also spent your life mostly doing things you know how to do well. Or, in the rare instances when you do try something new, you make up reasons why the circumstances made you bad at something. For example, the floor was uneven, so you tripped when you were trying to dance.

If the change you want to make is significant, you're going to be swimming in waters you've never been in before. You're going to have to open up to those around you and share that you're unhappy. You're going to have to say that things aren't what they seem and you want something different. All scary.

You're going to have to begin to do things in new and different ways for this change to succeed. It takes courage. Heck, even if you're just looking for a new job, you have to put yourself out there to see if anyone is interested in your experience and expertise.

Without vulnerability, there can be no "new." It's that simple.

WHAT YOU CAN DO

When you've built up your armor over years (or decades), being vulnerable can be terrifying. I get it. The first steps can be the hardest — and also necessary and sometimes surprisingly beautiful. Start by acknowledging your vulnerability and learning to ask for help. You will be surprised by how life-changing these steps can be.

Acknowledge Vulnerability

For me, vulnerability showed up when my brain was no longer able to function as quickly as it used to. It showed up when I returned to work, and I couldn't say my B's and P's. (note my name: Becca Pearce). It showed up when I had to ask my neighbors to take me for walks three times a day for the first month after surgery so I could relearn to walk. My vulnerability was forced upon me; I had no choice but to acknowledge it. It was not only acknowledging it but also embracing it that allowed me to move forward.

Had I not asked my neighbors for help, I wouldn't have been out learning to walk again. Had I waited to go back to work until I could pronounce my name, I would have been out of work for over a year — hiding from my realities. Going back to work forced me to do things that were difficult and made me vulnerable, but they also made me stronger. I was forced to practice my B's and P's, and I was forced to lead in my new reality. Without this, I would have never rebuilt myself and moved away from the perfectionist I used to be. Embracing those vulnerabilities allowed me to show up differently, be more human, and ultimately, see how vulnerability can make you stronger.

If you never embrace the vulnerability of trying something new, you will forever be stuck where you are today — unfortunately, aware that you're unhappy but too afraid to make a change.

It's time to let go. Let go of the belief that having no vulnerabilities makes you stronger. Let go of the belief that people want you to be perfect. Let go of the fear that others will see you as weak if you ask for help. Be brave, shed the armor you've built, and step into that space where you let others see you for you.

Ask For Help

Hah! Just typing that makes me laugh and cringe at the same time. How many overachievers know how to do this? Any? Not many, that's for sure. You've spent your life overachieving, not asking for help! How are you supposed to start asking for help now?

Just admitting that you need or want help is an act of bravery for those of you who have never asked for help before. Trust me, I was one of you. The surprising and amazing thing is you will find that other people *want* to help. In fact, your supporters have probably waited years for you to recognize they *can* help you and are happy to support you.

Your first step is to acknowledge that you can't do it all alone and that others can, indeed, help you. Next, choose someone you trust, open up to them, and let them help you.

You are, unfortunately, aware that you are not happy. But you can't change yourself in a vacuum. If your family and friends are used to you acting in a certain way, you need to let them know that something has shifted inside of you, and you want to make a change. You need to start the conversation because they can't read your mind. And they can't be a part of the solution until you tell them where you are.

I suggest starting by saying that you're doing something that's uncomfortable for you. If your loved ones know you're putting yourself out there, they will respond accordingly. I promise. Remember, if they love you, they will want the best for you. And if you're ready to acknowledge you want to change, the best thing you can do is find the courage to step into the uncomfortable so you can find a new comfortable.

These two steps — acknowledging vulnerability and asking for help — are the first steps of your outward change. They are the first signal to others that you want something new. They require courage, but if you don't take these steps, you'll stay exactly where you are today — sad and stuck.

JOURNAL REFLECTIONS

For people who have never embraced vulnerability before, hiding your truths is a way of life. So much so that you may not even realize you've been hiding them. This is you if you hear yourself saying things like: "It's fine." "Whatever." "I don't need them." This is a sign that you're pushing away a need and covering up a vulnerability.

Reflect here to help identify exactly what you want to say to your trusted person and plan your conversation. Ask yourself:

1. What truth (vulnerability) am I hiding from others on a regular basis?

2. What specific change do I want to ask for help with?

3. Who can I open up to about the change I want to make?

4. What do I want them to hear?

5. What do I need from them?

UNFORTUNATE AWARENESS SUMMARY

In the previous three chapters, you dove headfirst into the water you've been swimming in for years. You went deep into your own core belief — one that has driven you to overachieve — and now realize that being invulnerable can make you less likable and keep you unable to change. You've taken a closer look at how you spend your time and explored ways to change the trajectory of the future.

By understanding your own version of You Don't Have to Achieve to be Loved, you've begun to understand how you got to where you are (in addition to all that hard work, dedication, and blood, sweat, and tears.) You've come to see that while this belief has driven your career, achievements, and ambition, it hasn't landed you on a path to happiness.

Once you acknowledge that the belief that has been driving you for years *isn't true*, change becomes possible. Once you recognize that time is fleeting, you have the urgency to make the change you've been dreaming of. And now that you know the most important step you can take is to lean into your vulnerability, you are on your way out of Unfortunate Awareness and ready for the next phase.

I firmly believed my title and achievements were what made me worthy of love and would ultimately bring me happiness. I never gave a thought to time and how I was spending it (and I certainly never wondered if there was enough of it unless it was related to work). I thought that vulnerability meant weakness.

These notions kept me on that success train, going faster and faster, unable to get off, even though I wasn't happy — until I was forced to.

It was only when my mind was blown through these realizations that I recognized that I don't have to achieve to be loved, and my title doesn't matter. The only thing that truly matters is being available for my family.

My goal is for you to come to these realizations without having to go through what I did. Your job is to take what you've learned so far and use it to move you out of Unfortunate Awareness into the next phase.

JOURNAL REFLECTIONS

Now that you have worked through the first phase, let's see if your beliefs and opinions have started to shift. Find your journal and write your thoughts on the questions below.

1. What have you learned?

2. What preconceived notions do you have about your current world that you may be beginning to question?

3. Go back and review your journal entries and write about how they all come together.

4. What pieces of these perceptions will you keep? What no longer fits?

5. What will you commit to changing now so you can move forward in a new way?

Mourning the Past

I miss the
old me.

CURIOSITY

Something is
wrong.

COURAGE

2. Mourning the
Past

PERSONAL
BEHAVIORS

1. Unfortunate
Awareness

PERSONAL
EXPECTATIONS

MOURNING THE PAST

Mourning the Past is an interesting phase, and it's what most people go into immediately following Unfortunate Awareness. At this point, while you may have realized you aren't happy with the life you've been living, you can't reconcile those feelings with the person you've been your entire life. If you're unhappy, does that mean you don't like the person you were? The person who got you here? This is especially true for successful, accomplished people who have spent their whole lives proving their worth.

What You May Be Feeling

If you've done the soul-searching required in Phase 1, you are most likely now in this weird place where you can't decide if you like the "you" that got you here. But a part of you still loves, respects, and appreciates that person! These are odd feelings to balance.

Sometimes, my clients get mad at me for getting them into this position, and I get it. I asked them to look in the mirror and challenged them to think differently — to look at their past life and dissect it with a new lens. I understand their frustration because it's not a comfortable place to be. But stick with me!

The trick in this next stage is to be able to look at your past life and NOT DEMONIZE IT. The you that got you to where you are now is beautiful and loved and deserves to be appreciated! The you that got you here was strong and purposeful! You are still you, and there are core pieces of that person that will stay with you forever.

But if you've gotten this far, there are also pieces of the former you that you're ready to let go of. This is where mourning comes in.

You are mourning the person you were and the dreams that person had. However, you cannot make significant and lasting changes without letting go of something you were doing or the beliefs you held before.

I'm not saying it's easy. I'm saying it's necessary. This mourning is such a key part of sustainable change that if you don't go through it, your change either isn't significant or it won't stick.

So, bear with me through this part of the process.

Realizations

The realizations in this phase are the ones that had to be pounded into my brain for them to stick. They are also the ones that finally allowed me to stop lamenting who I was and what I thought I had lost. They're the ones that help clients open their eyes to the possibility of a different future. They are the ones that will allow you to move through mourning and into the next phase.

The realizations we'll discuss in this phase include:

- You Are Not Your Job
- Your Values Can Change
- It's Okay to Want Something New

Curiosity

Curiosity is an important quality for navigating this phase. You'll need to tap into your curiosity to look closely at the behaviors that got you where you are and think about what you need to let go of. You'll have to ask yourself questions like, "Why am I wishing for the old when I know I want the new?" and "What about my former self still appeals to me?"

This part of the book will help you appreciate who you have been while embracing the person you are becoming. They *can* coexist! It's curiosity that will lead you through this process — curiosity to explore more of your preconceived notions, curiosity about how to reconcile the old you and the new you, and curiosity to see what is possible and who you can be.

By the end of this phase, who you were before and who you are yet to become will begin to coexist for you.

If you want something new,
you need to stop doing something old.
— PETER DRUCKER

YOU ARE NOT YOUR JOB

Many successful people define themselves by what they do. It's very common but not particularly healthy. It's important to learn to separate who you are from what you do in order to move toward the changes you seek.

In my situation, when I was at the Exchange, I believed I *was* Obamacare in the state of Maryland. Read that again. I believed *I* was Obamacare in the state of Maryland. Like *all* of it — as if there weren't a gazillion other people in the state focused on Obamacare, and Obamacare didn't have a gazillion other pieces associated with it. Go ahead and laugh at me. A decade later, I can chuckle at it.

Some may think this is ego (and maybe there was a little of that), but it was really driven by the magnitude of the task and how important I thought the work was. If we succeeded, up to one million Marylanders would have access to healthcare, which they'd never had before. That's a huge deal.

There was also a lot of external pressure. I had a governor and lieutenant governor who both had greater aspirations. It was clear that a successful launch of the Exchange was vital to those aspirations. I felt like I had the world on my shoulders every minute of every day.

And if that wasn't enough, the PRESIDENT OF THE UNITED STATES was depending on our success to show the country that this vital piece of the ACA could work.

So, it's no wonder I felt the magnitude of the task in front of me.

During those two years, I was in the news regularly. I spoke publicly at every meeting we had, testified before the Maryland legislature at least fifteen times over two legislative sessions, and met with every state legislator who had a say in what we were doing. At one point, I had to stand up to the CEO of an IBM corporation and a room full of men, all older than me, and tell them to "stop f***ing" with the government's money. I was named one of the fifty most interesting women by the *Baltimore Sun* and one of thirteen to watch in 2013 by *The Daily Record*.

You can see how I started to feel like I was important.

As it turns out, nothing about this was related to *me*. It was all related to the position I held. But I didn't see that at the time. I had conflated the two. I had also failed to see that "CEO of the Maryland Health Benefit Exchange" had become my identity. I was too close to it. I lived and breathed it. I *was* it, remember?

I had lost myself to the job.

So, when the call came that fateful Friday afternoon in December, and I was forced to walk away from all of it, I was dazed. I didn't see it coming. I had been so committed, and I thought I was still making a difference. I was angry, sad that I didn't get to see it through, and worried that people would think I had given up.

And I didn't know who I was without the title.

WHY THIS MATTERS

If you're an overachiever, a perfectionist, or just highly successful, you can probably relate to my story. There's a good chance you, too, identify yourself by your successes and/or job title. If so, you have an identity issue that needs to be resolved. You will likely mourn that part of who you were.

If your identity is tied to something completely different, like your kids or your spouse, there's good information in this chapter for you as well, so keep reading.

Stripping away that old identity — whatever it's tied to — is one of the hardest things to do. I'm not going to lie. It hurts (especially when it's been stripped from you like it was for me). But even if you are making the decision on your own to change something, an important part of your identity is shifting. This will be one of the hardest parts of the journey.

Shifting away from your old identity is also one of the most vital actions you must take when moving through this stage. Without this mourning phase, you cannot let go of the image of what was — how great it was, how you saw yourself in its greatness, and how you believed you'd found happiness. Without this shift, you will never move forward and create meaningful, sustainable change.

Why Do I See Myself This Way?

Identifying ourselves by what we do has some deep roots.

Let's start with childhood. When asked about our dreams for the future, we were usually asked, "What do you want to be when you grow up?" Note the language — "What do you want to BE?" not "What do you want to DO?" From the beginning, society tells us that what we do for a job or living is tied to who we are.

Going back in history, you find that many common surnames were given specifically because of the job someone held (Smith, Miller, Baker, Fisher, etc.). You might not have ever associated these names with a job, but that's how they originated, and this is another example of how ingrained these things are in our society.

If you go back just a generation or two, people had little or no choice about what they did for a living — they worked in factories or took over their family's business. For them, a job was a job; it wasn't an identity like it can be for some today.

Today, with more choices in careers, when someone asks you what you do, your response can signify to the other person your social status and/or your wealth. As Anne Wilson, professor of psychology at Wilfred Laurier University in Ontario, says in a BBC article, "That is especially true among the 'educated elite.' For people who have a certain type of job and certain class, it often becomes how you identify yourself and how others identify you."[10]

Let's expand upon that social status piece and how change is scary for people who have identified with their role. Who are you if you aren't the business owner, executive, or leader you were? One of the most common things my clients worry about when they are about to retire is relevance. The joke is, "Hi, I'm Sally. I used to be important."

Finally, when we're meeting people for the first time, what's one of the first questions out of your mouth? "What do you do?" Bam! You're connecting job to identity. Ask anyone who doesn't have a job outside the home how hard it is to answer that question, and you'll have a better understanding of just how much our culture ties identity to what we do.

So, it's not surprising that we define ourselves by our jobs. It's rooted in history, ingrained in us from a young age, and fanned by societal norms.

Enmeshment

Psychologists actually have a name for this. It's called enmeshment.

When you tie your identity to your job, boundaries become unclear. According to J.H Westover, with enmeshment, "an individual's professional identity takes over their personal identity. This means that they become so closely identified with their job that their personal interests, values, and hobbies take a back seat."[11]

Do you find the only thing you talk about is work? Do you think about work constantly? Do you have a hard time associating with anyone outside of work? When was the last time you did something for fun or with nonwork people? And when's the last time you did that without checking your phone for an email?

Enmeshment is a vicious circle. Working all the time (or even just thinking about work all the time) makes it hard to relate to people you don't work with. When work is all-consuming, you give up hobbies and non-work friends. Without those, your world shrinks further, and you have nothing to talk about besides work. So, you work even more because you've lost everything else. Work is all you know and soon becomes your whole identity.

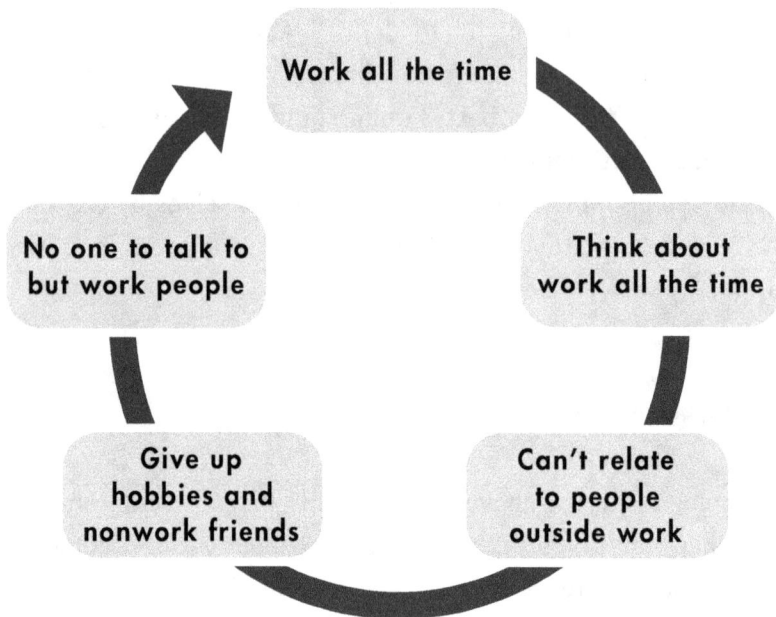

What Is the Impact of This?

There are very real consequences with this kind of skewed thinking about identity. When talking about the mental health effects, Tom Fryers describes its impact on our personal identity, saying, "Without a clear sense of personal identity, it is difficult to have the self-esteem we need to function well as independent people in an inter-dependent society... we are vulnerable to psychological injury, at risk of anxiety and depression, and social disengagement... we cannot easily respond to love with love, to accept forgiveness, to start again after failure."[12]

For many of my clients, enmeshment looks like this:

- Loss of any outside interests or hobbies
- Troubled relationships with spouses/partners and/or children/family
- Anxiety and/or depression
- Isolation from friends
- Lack of personal fulfillment
- Weight gain
- Burn-out

Further, clients who have lost their jobs and, therefore, feel they've lost their identity tend to experience one or all of the following:

- Total loss of self-esteem
- Inability to see what value they have to offer to any company or the world at large
- Difficulty presenting themselves intelligently in interviews
- Prolonged unemployment

WHAT YOU CAN DO

Set Boundaries

If you go back to the definition of enmeshment, you will see that it describes boundaries that have become unclear. When what you do becomes who you are, your boundaries with your job are too intertwined. For many of my clients, those boundaries just don't exist.

The good news is it's never too late to set some boundaries! Boundaries come in many forms. They can be hard or soft; they can apply to everyone, or they can apply to only certain people. They can apply in all situations or just some situations.

It's important to note that boundaries are not something you put on other people. They are actions you take to hold space for yourself. Let me give you a few examples of boundaries my clients have set for themselves over the years:

- Not checking email after 7:00 p.m.
- Going to all your children's home soccer games
- Always answering the phone for family
- Not emailing staff after midnight

These boundaries have enabled my clients to begin to get their lives back. **What boundaries could you put into place to begin your separation?**

Decide Who You Want to Be

"Who do you want to be?" I know this is a very "coachy" question. But when we ask you who you want to be, we're really asking you what *type of person* you want to be. I want to be a person who ___. Common responses I get to this question are someone who:

- doesn't work twelve hours a day
- has time and energy for family
- responds to friends when they text
- has at least one hobby outside of work

- gives back
- is nice(!)

When you shift your identity from what you do to who you are, you begin to recognize all the facets of your life. Instead of your title, what you do, or what you've achieved, you begin to focus on the type of person you are and the one you hope to be.

Reflect And Assess

Do you think your current level of enmeshment increases the value of the work you do? Many of my clients think there's a direct correlation. I'm here to tell you that's a fallacy. The truth is, the more enmeshed you are, the less perspective you have. The more you work, the less space there is for your brain to be creative, and the more likely you are to make mistakes.

And equally significant, the more you work, the more likely it is you're putting your physical health at risk. A study conducted by the World Health Organization concluded that working 55 hours or more per week is associated with an estimated 35 percent higher risk of a stroke and a 17 percent higher risk of dying from heart disease compared to working 35 to 40 hours per week.[13]

What sorts of errors are you making because you're overworked, and what impact is overworking having on your health? What effect is this having on your relationships? Quick answer? More than you realize and more than you'd like.

You are not your job.

You are more than your job.

There's a chance you have lost sight of that fact, and that's okay. You can find yourself again if you reassess how you invest your time and energy, figure out who you want to be, and learn to set boundaries.

I have seen many of my clients take these steps to find their identities outside of their jobs again. You can do it too.

JOURNAL REFLECTIONS

As mentioned above, the key steps toward separating yourself from your job include understanding how you want to invest your time and energy, defining the type of person you want to be, and setting boundaries to support this new time investment. Journal about all three of these topics by asking yourself:

1. Boundaries
   a. What boundaries do I currently have in place when it comes to work?
   b. What boundaries do I want to add?
   c. What will those boundaries change for me?

2. Fill in the blank: I want to be a person who _____. Write down as many things as come to your mind. Then, write about how you can begin to make this happen.

3. Reflect on and assess how much time you currently work and what value those additional hours are really providing. (Note: I strongly recommend that you do some real analysis here. Look at your calendar and calculate your time for the month. Without data, our brains can create any story.)

YOUR VALUES CAN CHANGE

You might feel like it will be impossible to make the type of changes we've been talking about. At the same time, you know deep down that something isn't right, and you want something different. It's time to revisit your core values.

I've done core values exercises twice — once when I was training to get my coaching certificate and then again as I was working on my strategic business plan. In both instances, I was post-surgery, had already quit my job, and had decided I wanted something different. But one of the two times was when I was still hanging on to the old me with all my might. The other was when I had finally let go and become the person I am now.

In the first round (again, while I was still mourning the old me), I identified the following as my core values:

1. Hard work
2. Strength
3. Perseverance
4. Tenacity
5. Challenge

I loved these core values. They said I was strong!

Interestingly, if you look very closely underneath these, you will see I still clearly believed achievement was the key to my happiness. It wasn't until one of my coaches asked me how these fit into my everyday life that I began to realize they didn't really fit me anymore. They were the values I had learned growing up and the ones that had made me success-ful my entire career. Part of me still valued them (and still does), but they didn't fit anymore. I had changed. The things I cared about had changed. And these were no longer the val-ues that drove me every day.

I had developed a new perspective about what was im-portant to me. When I really began to embrace the new me, I realized my family and being with my family outweighed every-thing else in my life now. If there was a toss-up between work-ing harder on a project and spending time with Elaina, Elaina won hands down every time.

I was also softer and gentler. I cared more about listening to others and hearing what they had to say rather than being heard. I was more comfortable asking for help and recognized that sometimes strength is asking for help instead of trying to do it all alone.

Working with this coach, I repeated the core values exercise and came up with the following:

1. Family
2. Balance
3. Hearing Others
4. Growth
5. Kind directness

These values show up in my life every day, without fail. They drive all my decisions, both personal and professional. They are core to my business and how I treat my clients, and they remind me why I do what I do.

WHY THIS MATTERS

Your core values are the basis of your soul. They are the fundamental principles and beliefs a person or organization considers to be most important. Your core values underpin every decision you make and every action you take, whether you realize it or not. If you have two in conflict, the stronger core value will pull you to your ultimate decision.

And these values can change. The core values you had in the past may not be the ones you want to carry with you into the future. Understanding and claiming your core values are key aspects of moving forward.

This realization — that your core values can change — comes in the mourning phase as you continue to move away from who you were toward who you are becoming. This phase is marked by constant questioning about what you're leaving behind (often with rose-colored glasses that now make that past seem amazing and wonderful!).

As you realize that the values that got you this far aren't necessarily the values you still hold, you start to understand that maybe you're different — maybe that person you were was great for then, but this is now. It's this realization that allows the new you to begin to coexist with the old you and allows you to move through mourning into the next phase.

Where Do Core Values Come From?

Similar to many of the things we've discussed, you are a product of your upbringing. So, it should come as no surprise that your core values are entrenched early on. Similar to beliefs, values most often come from your family, education, culture, society, and community.

As a child, you absorb everything around you and instinctively learn what values will keep you safe. For example, if your parent says you're lazy if you sit down to read a book, you will value movement over reading. Those values, then, become the ones you carry with you until at least your teen years. It's as a teenager that you begin to forge your own way, start to look at things differently, and gain a sense of self that's separate from your family. At that point, there's a good chance your values will shift, but they are always informed by your personal history.

Your teachers also play a role in helping form your values by reinforcing certain beliefs, attitudes, and behaviors. In fact, research has shown that "the education system is one of the 'most efficient institutions to teach human values to the next generations in the community.'"[14] This is because much of our time in our formative years is spent in learning institutions, and, as we know, many of our values are formed in these early years.

These values are further reinforced in your immediate community. You quickly learn about right and wrong based on reactions within your community.

There is also a cultural influence. We are all born into a set of values that shape the beliefs and behaviors of an entire culture. For example, Japan places a strong emphasis on social harmony and avoiding conflict. In the United States, we have been taught to strive for "The American Dream," which can result in placing value on achievement and success over other things. (More on this topic later!)

Changing Values Isn't Easy

We've established how important core values are and that they can, indeed, change. But it's not always easy. That's why this part of the journey — Mourning the Past — is so difficult.

Maggie Wooll, author, speaker, and former lead researcher at the Deloitte Center for the Edge, describes it as follows: "Once you hit adulthood, it's more difficult to change your values. It's not impossible, but the problem is that changing your values usually involves questioning core parts of your identity. Learning to put family before your career would require an examination and adjustment of your personal ambitions and sense of self."[15]

You, my friend, are smack dab in the middle of this right now. Core values can and do change! Doing the hard work of looking very closely at yours will allow you to define exactly what drives you today.

When Core Values Aren't Aligned

If you feel frustrated, triggered, or angry about something, there's a good chance one of your core values is being tromped on.

Andrew, a client, was terribly unhappy at his job, and he didn't know why. He was in a position that suited him, and he loved the external-facing aspects of his job. But he still was not happy at work. I had him do the core value exercise, and his results were as follows:

1. Generosity
2. Kindness
3. Respect
4. Trust
5. Acknowledgment
6. Loyalty

I then asked him to tell me what the company's core values were. He listed:

1. Tackle Hard Problems
2. Be the Catalyst
3. Seek Clarity
4. Take Ownership
5. Accelerate Clock Speed
6. Find a Better Way

You can probably see the issue as clearly as I do. It's not surprising that he was miserable! Those values couldn't be much further apart. Everything the organization valued was related to pushing harder and being assertive, while my client valued collaboration and respect. His personal values were being challenged on a daily basis, and that made him feel terrible.

WHAT YOU CAN DO

One way to start is by doing a core values assessment. You can find at least twenty of them online just by Googling "core values assessment." Each assessment will be slightly different. Their word lists will be different, or they'll have a different set of reflection questions. Pick an assessment that seems right for you and take it. For the version I use with my clients, go to YouDontHaveToAchieveToBeLoved.com.

No matter how many words the assessment lets you pick, winnow your list down to the top five values. Only five. I understand that this is a hard process, but it's essential that you pick the five that are most important to you so you can focus on what really matters.

Next, rank the five values in order of their importance to you.

Now, look at the list and ask yourself how these values show up in your life every day. If one or more are not evident at all, you may have missed the mark on your list. For example, if "health" is on your list, but you're not making time to work out, meditate, go to the doctor, or take care of your health in some other way, then health is not really a core value. You should revisit the possible values or consider trying a different assessment.

Then, ask yourself where these values came from. Are they yours, or are they someone else's? Sometimes, the core values you have may also be the ones your family shares. If you're in the process of change, you may realize that your core values have begun to shift.

Once you've completed the steps above, take your current core values and post them somewhere you can see them every day. Mine are on my bulletin board, written out beautifully by

Elaina. I look at them regularly and am proud to say I am living my life according to my values. This exercise may still seem silly or inconsequential, but **identifying and regularly reviewing your core values can change your life.**

JOURNAL REFLECTIONS

Outside of the core values exercises, there are other ways to identify some of your core values. For example, we are often drawn to people who share our core values, so looking at your relationships could help identify some of your values. Also, when we see ourselves at our best, it's because we are exemplifying our core values. Use these prompts to begin your core values work.

1. What draws you to your closest friends?

2. What is the common denominator between you and these friends?

3. What do you do when you feel most free to be yourself? Who are you when you're most free?

4. Write about a time you were at your best. What is it about this story that has you saying you were at your best? What values do you recognize in that story?

IT'S OKAY TO WANT SOMETHING NEW

Exploring what you truly value can open up new possibilities and raise new questions. You might begin to see the disconnect between what you value and what you're doing. This is not uncommon! And yet, you may continue to wonder if it's okay to want something different than what you've been striving for your whole life.

After surgery, I had to prove to myself that I could do my job again. I had spent my entire life believing title and achievement mattered, and immediately post-surgery, that belief hadn't changed. But more importantly, I had to prove that the brain tumor hadn't won. I had to prove that I *could* be the person I was before.

When I returned to work, it was not easy. I still had trouble saying my B's and P's; my left hand was too shaky and unreliable to type effectively (or even scratch my face without poking myself in the eye, if I'm being honest); my brain was working so hard to keep me upright that I couldn't effectively walk and talk at the same time; and I fell asleep with my shoes on when I came home because I was so tired.

But each day, I slowly improved. I re-engaged with projects that had moved forward while I was out. I sat in meetings and asked questions that would challenge the people in the room to think bigger. I took copious notes to make sure my brain captured everything that was going on. I even took on new projects to lead efforts around employee engagement.

After several months, I was doing the job again — running meetings, keeping up with everything going on around me, and adding value. I was doing everything I had wanted to prove I could do.

I had done it!

So, I was a little surprised that instead of feeling elated, only one thought kept replaying in my mind, "Why?" Why was I putting myself back into the stress of being a VP? Why was I struggling to get out of the house in the morning in time for a meeting when I knew, without a doubt, that the only thing that mattered to me was putting Elaina on the bus one more time?

It was at this moment that I realized something had changed. I didn't want the success train I'd been on for years. I wanted something new. I wanted to have the freedom to be with my family at all costs because I knew now that this was the only thing that mattered in my life. And while this knowledge was crystal clear to me, I wasn't exactly sure what to do with this realization. I did know, though, that the idea of a different way of life had taken hold.

This is how I found myself walking into work on a crisp morning in February, talking to Ed on the phone about wanting to quit my job. It was a tense conversation. We had discussed why I wanted to quit my job before, but on this day, I was certain it *needed* to happen.

He understood that I wanted a change, but we were coming from two different places. Ed is practical. He loves routine and relishes security. I was the breadwinner in the family, and letting go of that income and security was not an easy idea to reconcile. But things had changed. *I* had changed.

I wanted and needed something new in my life. I no longer wanted to be in the role I was in. I wanted more time to spend with Ed and Elaina and the space to become someone new. It had taken me months to give myself permission to want something new and to decide what to do with my realization. Now that I had that permission, I needed to make it a reality.

As I walked up the building's steps, Ed asked, "Could you hang on for another year or two?" I looked at myself in the mirrored glass of the building and said to him, **"What if I'm not alive in two years?"**

Two hours later, I quit my job.

WHY THIS MATTERS

I worked for years to climb the corporate ladder and get to the top. After the Exchange, I reinvented myself within the same space and continued down the same path I had put myself on years ago. Post-surgery, I worked insanely hard to prove to myself that I could do the job again — all in an effort to get back on that same track and continue my trajectory. The thought of giving up all of that hard work and not striving for the next title or responsibility had never crossed my mind. When it did, it felt almost blasphemous. I had worked so hard for this. How could I just not want it anymore?

It took months for me to come to terms with this shift in thinking, and I suspect the same may be true for you. If you're successful, you've likely spent years building that success. The thought of never achieving your original goal or of walking away from the future you had envisioned for yourself is a hard pill to swallow. But you're here because something isn't working, and you have a sense you want something different. You may not know what's next, but you know you do not want to be where you are right now. Your dreams have changed. I'm here to tell you that's okay. It's okay to want something new!

Acceptance Is a Process

Learning to accept that you want this change is a process. In Unfortunate Awareness, you know something isn't right, but for many of my clients, the thought of giving up what they've spent years building toward is something they can't fathom.

This is where the mourning phase comes into play. Peter Drucker says, "If you want to start doing something new, you have to stop doing something old."[16] For you, wanting something new means having to give up or let go of something old — your former goals or dreams. The mourning phase is not only mourning the old you but also the dreams you had.

I had wanted to be a CEO again. In my process, I had to come to terms with the fact that being a CEO might never happen if I made this change. It was only after I accepted that fact that I was able to give myself permission to move on. You will need to do the same. It's often very hard to let go of those dreams. But the interesting thing is that there must be a part of you that doesn't really want those dreams anymore; otherwise, you wouldn't be here.

It's important to mourn the person you were as well as the old dreams. It's equally important to begin to look toward what's possible and who you can be. This is your moment to figure out how you want to be remembered, what you hope your legacy will be, and what really matters to you. This is your opportunity to redefine who you are and what your future will hold.

Don't Regret Your Future

The change you're thinking about may feel big and scary. You can probably think of multiple reasons (excuses) why you shouldn't make the change. But please don't let these fears stop you; don't let current excuses become a future regret.

Research shows two main facts when it comes to regret: The first is that the larger the missed opportunity, the greater the likelihood of future regret.[17] The second is that feelings of regret in the long term are more likely to come from decisions involving inaction (choosing *not* to do something).[18]

In fact, if you do a quick search of people's biggest regrets in life, you will find they often include:[19]

- Not spending enough time with loved ones
- Working too much
- Not living my own life — living my life for others
- Not taking more risks
- Not prioritizing my health

See how most of these regrets are related to something NOT done or a risk NOT taken?

I bet at least one of these regrets hits close to home for you. You may have even reacted when you read the list because of regrets about a decision you've already made or are currently making.

Identifying what could potentially become your biggest regret can provide insight into what you really want to change. Get curious about the future you're designing. Think about your motivations. How will things be different if you allow yourself to want something new and actually make the change you want? What regrets will you have if you DON'T make this change?

Your Brain Wants to Keep You Safe

Perhaps you're currently trying to convince yourself that you can't possibly take the leap you've been dreaming about. This is partially because your brain is screaming for you to stay safe.

Among the many functions of the human brain, the most important is to keep us safe. It will always err on the side of security and will trigger the fight-or-flight response when it senses a threat. Similarly, if you listen to the voices in your head, you'll notice that those voices also tend to try to keep you from doing things that are risky or could make you vulnerable. This biological programming, intended to keep us safe, explains why we like to stick with what we know and avoid choices that include risk. It's why so many people stay the course — and then regret it later.

This is why, if you realize you no longer want that future, you're likely to feel conflicted. Remember how our neural pathways are set? Our experiences and beliefs create specific neural pathways that default to the choices that have been made in the past (the safe path). But these pathways can be changed, and you can create new ones when envisioning your new future. **Where in your life are you choosing security over taking a risk?**

Use curiosity to look closely at your situation. What is the disconnect between what you want to do and what you're doing now? What is your brain saying to you to keep you in place? (Feel free to stop and write all the things your brain is telling you about why you shouldn't make the change you want.)

Conflict Between Old and New

As you lean into this change and allow your perspective to morph, you're likely to feel a pull between the old and new. Don't be afraid of the tension; it's an indicator that you're on the right track.

You're not stuck in a specific job or career. You can change your trajectory. People do it successfully every day. It's okay to want something new, even if you've spent years focused on the old and even if you're scared of what others will think. Everyone who truly loves you only wants you to be happy. Period. There are no caveats.

Meanwhile, as you begin to embrace what you want, it's normal to question whether this is a "grass is greener" situation or if what you're heading toward will actually make you happy. This shows you're thinking things through. But don't let this completely take over your thoughts — remember, your brain may be playing tricks on you! To try to alleviate this, do some research. Talk to someone in the space you're looking to enter. Find out if the grass is actually greener and if people are happy.

Happiness

Some people wonder if they will ever really know what makes them happy. Fortunately, researchers have spent a lot of time considering how to navigate change and find what brings us happiness and satisfaction. This information can help you prioritize what matters in life.

For instance, the Pew Research Center survey found that for U.S. adults, *family* was the most common source of meaning and satisfaction. That study also found there were four areas of life that were universally associated with higher levels of life meaning and satisfaction: *good health, romantic partner, career, and friends.*[20] The more you find meaning in these areas, the happier and more satisfied you are overall.

Similarly, the longest-running study in history, the Harvard Study of Adult Development, has followed the same cohort of 724 men for over seventy-five years, studying their happiness, health, and well-being. The participants were from varying socioeconomic and educational backgrounds, yet the single most important factor across the board for individual happiness and health was *relationships.* The study found that those who are most connected to family and friends live longer and are overall healthier and happier.[21] Think about that for a minute — the quality of your personal relationships has a direct impact on your health and longevity.

So What?

While it's part of the picture, work is not the entire picture; it's finding meaning in that work that increases satisfaction and happiness. However, this is only true when it's balanced with other aspects of your life. In fact, working too long and too hard is one of the most common regrets.

In addition, solid family and personal relationships contribute to a happier and healthier life. It took public humiliation and a brain tumor for me to realize I needed to find a new career — one that fed my soul while allowing me to focus on the relationships that were most important to me. My hope for you in reading this book is that you notice these things now.

WHAT YOU CAN DO

You might feel like you've worked your entire life to get where you are. You may feel like you are making "good money." Or maybe you're running the business your father left you. Even when these things are true, you can still feel like something isn't right. Even if your identity is tied to what you're doing now, you can still be unhappy with your current situation. If this is the case, it's likely because what you're doing doesn't actually align with your current values or core needs. It doesn't feed your soul or give you meaning.

It's okay to want something different than what you have right now! Understanding this and embracing your new dreams will move you out of the Mourning the Past phase and into the future you're designing.

Stuck

After working with hundreds of clients, I've found three common factors that can keep people stuck in a phase of mourning the past, afraid to give up what was.

The first factor I call the **outside-looking-in syndrome**. It shows up in phrases such as, "but I shouldn't complain, I have the freedom/income/etc. I want." From the outside, you have everything you should want: a good career, a cute family, a good house, and others would love to be in your situation, so you feel bad thinking you want something different. Meanwhile, on the inside, you're dying a slow death. The things you thought would make you happy aren't making you happy now. The image of what it would look like if you made a change keeps you stuck in mourning, thinking you're giving up something others would love to have. But do they really think that? You actually have no idea.

I call the second factor **the freedom handcuffs**. You've spent years getting to a point where there are *pieces* of your current situation that are amazing. Maybe you work from home, or no one looks over your shoulder at what you do on a daily basis. Maybe the lifestyle and financial freedom you've grown accustomed to would go away if you made a drastic change.

For some people, it's hard to see past these things because these "freedoms" often buy them some aspects of their lives that they love. When this is the case, they sometimes choose to tolerate their dissatisfaction, worrying that if they give up these things, dissatisfaction will only increase. But will it? What if they could find these things again and make a change at the same time?

The third factor is slightly different. **Many people know what they *don't* want, but most don't know what they *do* want.**

Part of this is societal. I'm going to generalize here, but with good reason. Throughout history, women have been taught not to make waves and to make everyone else in the room feel comfortable (and look good doing it!). As a result, most of the women I coach have spent their entire lives focused on what other people want and need, relegating their own needs to the bottom rung.

Men have been taught to be the knights in shining armor who provide for the family, hide emotions, and hold everything together. Most of the men I coach have spent their entire careers focused on providing for the family, worried about their income, and pushing toward the next promotion. These societal roles make it difficult for people to see what it is that they truly want.

All three of these common factors let you convince yourself that the benefits of your current situation are worth it and that you shouldn't want more. This mindset doesn't allow you to give yourself the space to consider and understand what you actually want. But the truth is, everyone deserves to live a life that makes them happy. The next sections will give you an opportunity to envision change in your life.

Getting Unstuck

To get unstuck, I want to take you through a reflection used by a colleague of mine with his financial planning clients. It's meant to help clients identify what matters most to them. Today, you're going to do the same!

To get started, find a quiet space and imagine the following: **You just received notice that you are going to die within the year. You aren't going to be sick, and you don't know the date, but you know you have 365 days or less to live.**

What would you change?

Of course, it's unrealistic to live our lives thinking we're going to die within the year — but stay with me for a moment and truly imagine it.

Immediately, I'm going to assume you say, "Well, I'd quit my job." I mean, who doesn't say that, right? (Interestingly, if you say you would quit your job, doesn't that say something about its importance in your life overall? It seems important, but is it really in the long run?)

So, say you would quit your job. What would you do? Travel? Spend time with your family and friends? Reflect now on what you would do and get specific — really specific. Would you take your child out of school for the travel you're envisioning? If you want to take that trip to Africa but your child would miss the musical they've been practicing for, would you go? With or without them? What if your partner had to keep working?

We dream of things we would love to do. But the reality is life happens around us, and some dreams just can't become reality. This exercise forces you to look death in the face (without really having to look death in the face) and see what's actually important to you.

If you chose Africa over the musical, then traveling and seeing the world is important to you. If you chose the musical because you couldn't imagine not being there, you know your family is the most important thing.

If this were your last year on the planet, what would you regret about the life you've lived? What would you change?

This chapter is about giving yourself permission to want something new. The exercise is meant to help you recognize what really matters to you. It's meant to give you space to identify the things you want to be different. What do you want to change moving forward? If you see a disconnect between what you would change and how you're living today (even a small one), let's work together to connect the two.

Change

Now that you've imagined a shortened future and identified what matters most, what do you want that's new? What needs to change? Keep that in mind as we continue forward.

Remember that not all changes you make have to be sweeping, elaborate, or even noticeable to others to make a difference in your life. The change simply needs to redirect you to what matters most.

Change can be something as small as smiling at someone you pass on the street, noticing little things around you, or changing the way you react to something that has previously bothered you. It can be taking more control over when you choose to respond to an email. Maybe it's committing to meet a friend for dinner when you've been too busy to do it in the past. When you know what matters, it's impossible not to want to do something about it right away.

If you realized during the exercise above that you would go to your child's school, find the time to go one day this school year. If you realized you would like to spend more time with your parents, then make plans to see them in the next three months. If you realized you haven't told your partner you love them recently, tell them you love them tonight.

Yes, it's that simple to start the process. It's that simple to begin to change the neural pathways that have gotten you to where you are today. Small steps like these will help you see what actually matters in life and what drives your happiness. You will also be surprised to know this is the beginning of bigger realizations and more clarity about where you want to go.

Prior to this part of the process, many clients feel they are running away from something. At this point, they begin to realize they are running toward new possibilities. By embracing new dreams, even if you've spent years focused on past dreams, you're opening up a world of possibilities, which allows you to stop mourning what was.

JOURNAL REFLECTIONS

Mourning the Past and holding on to stability are natural responses to change. It feels safer to keep doing what you've been doing. And yet, you are in the process of allowing yourself to want something new and taking action to make that a reality. Take a few moments to reflect on the prompts below to create your immediate path forward.

1. Define for yourself what your big-picture change is. Note: You may have already defined this! Rewrite at least part of it here.

2. Now, think about what interim changes will have to take place to meet your big-picture change.

3. What is the smallest step you can take to make a change now?

4. What will it impact?

5. How will you be different when you take this small step?

MOURNING THE PAST SUMMARY

Change does not happen by simply reading a chapter and moving on. It's a process that occurs gradually and is fueled by curiosity and self-reflection. It's earned through a keen self-awareness of what you want now versus what you wanted in the past. It happens when you finally come to peace with where the old and the new live symbiotically within you.

By Mourning the Past, you're preparing to let it go and move forward. You've spent time exploring your identity, values, and dreams and seen how they have changed.

You've accepted that something is missing or not quite right in your current situation. You've started to think about *who* you want to be instead of *what* you want to be, and you've identified your core values. You've come to see that your dreams can change.

Change can be hard. People generally don't change until the pain of staying where they are outweighs the pain of change. The Mourning the Past phase ends when you confidently know you are happier changing yourself and your life than staying the same.

Only when you reach this point can you begin to work through the pain of change with peace and dignity. You can begin to look at what got you to this point and selectively choose what you want to keep doing and what you want to let go of. You're discovering a new balance where who you were in the past can coexist with who you want to become.

I was able to create the best version of myself by taking the best parts of the old me and merging them with the new me. I love all the pieces of me I've kept and appreciate the parts I've let go that served me for a long time but don't anymore.

Now it's your turn to connect the pieces of yourself together to define how your dreams have changed and why your old dreams no longer support the future you want so that you can let go of pieces of the past that no longer suit you.

JOURNAL REFLECTIONS

As we complete the Mourning the Past phase, let's pause to reflect on how your mindset has shifted. Take a few moments to think about what that shift means for you and what's next.

1. Who are you outside of your job?

2. How are you living your values every day? What do you want to change to live within your values more?

3. What part of your old dream is no longer serving you?

4. Piece all of these together and write about what's coming up for you.

One Foot In, One Foot Out

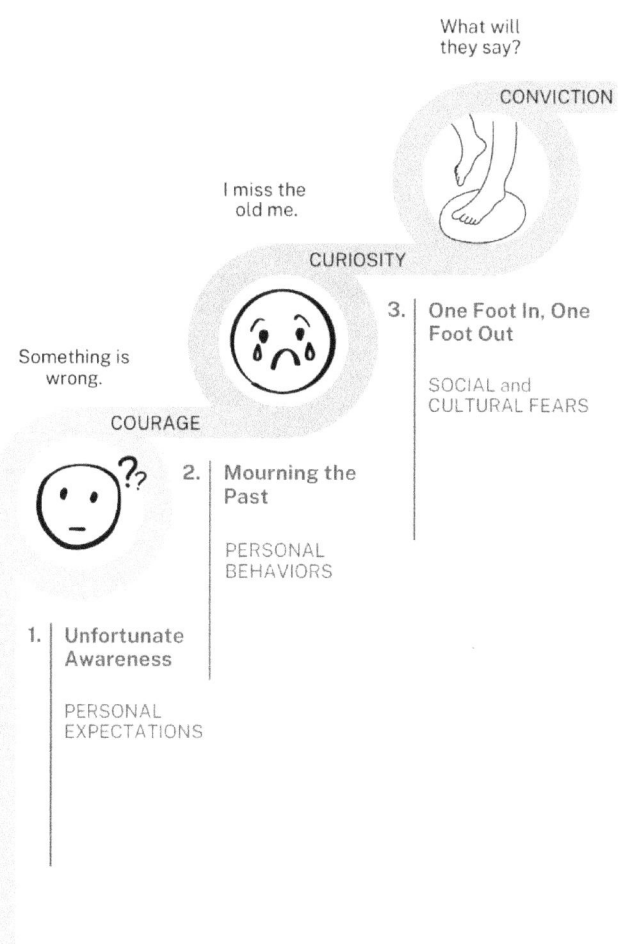

What will
they say?

CONVICTION

I miss the
old me.

CURIOSITY

3. One Foot In, One
Foot Out

SOCIAL and
CULTURAL FEARS

Something is
wrong.

COURAGE

2. Mourning the
Past

PERSONAL
BEHAVIORS

1. Unfortunate
Awareness

PERSONAL
EXPECTATIONS

ONE FOOT IN, ONE FOOT OUT

Imagine yourself at a beautiful lake where you're standing on a dock. You've set one foot in a boat, and the other remains firmly planted on the steady dock. The water is calm, and the boat is secure, but you're caught between the stability of the dock and the uncertainty of the boat. You hesitate and find yourself straddling the water, not sure which way to go. Back to safety or into the boat? Welcome to Phase 3: One Foot In, One Foot Out.

As a coach, I know that during this phase of your personal journey, you may be hovering in this hesitation and uncertainty. You want to feel the sea spray on your face, but stepping off that dock means leaving the safety of everything you've known for years. This leaves you with one foot on the safety of the dock and the other warily in the boat as you consider the broader impact of your changes. This is the definition of One Foot In, One

Foot Out — balancing the familiar with the new until you're ready to commit fully to a shift.

What You May Be Feeling

Up until this point, you've completed a lot of hard work on your own, identifying which pieces of you to keep and which no longer serve you. You've clearly defined your current values, understanding how these may have changed from what they used to be, and releasing old dreams so you can envision new ones.

Now, it's time to incorporate these personal changes into other aspects of your life. Your priorities have probably shifted, and it may feel scary to share this with others. You may ask yourself, "If I make this change, who will my friends be?" or "What will my family say?" or "What will people think of me?"

During the One Foot In, One Foot Out phase, you're beginning to dance with the idea of being a new person but may find yourself questioning the social aspects of who you are. Up until now, we have focused on you and what you want. Now, we're going to address the systems within which you operate.

No person is an island, and much of who you are is defined by your social systems, which provide you with safety and security. Therefore, it makes sense to question what may happen to them when you change.

Questioning how others may interpret your changes is the wind picking up, creating some chop on the water, and making it harder to decide if you can actually step into that boat. It's safer to stay on the dock with the social norms you're used to. It's connected to the land and a safe, known entity.

But deep down, you've wanted to get in this boat for a while. No one jumps into a major change without having thought about it on some level for a long time.

Realizations

The mind-blowing realizations in this phase will help you come to terms with the social ties that bind you to where you are today. You will see there's a good chance you've been living someone else's definition of success. You will learn how optimism can drive your future and when to use anger to your advantage. You will realize that relationships will run the course they're meant to run. Throughout this process, you will ultimately figure out that you want the change you've been seeking!

The realizations in this phase include:

- You've Been Living Someone Else's Definition of Success
- Optimism Is Your Friend (So Is Anger)
- You Will Find Your People

These concepts will help you step away from old habits and move toward where you want to go. They are the ideas that allowed me to finally let go of the person I was and embrace the person I have become. It wasn't until these realizations were solidified that I could make that leap. I share them in this book because they are not only my truths but also those of my clients.

Conviction

In this phase, you'll be guided by the conviction that the future you envision is worth this effort. You know this is the change you want. You will be pulled multiple times in multiple ways back to the safety of that dock, but lean into your conviction when you are questioning yourself. You know yourself better than anyone, and you know you want this! If you start to feel doubt creep in, remind yourself that you have the strength to see this through.

I promise you will be happier on the other side. You will step out of One Foot In, One Foot Out, knowing that getting in that boat is absolutely the right move for you.

YOU'VE BEEN LIVING SOMEONE ELSE'S DEFINITION OF SUCCESS

We are prone to judge success by the index of our salaries or the size of our automobiles rather than by the quality of our service and relationship to mankind.

— MARTIN LUTHER KING JR.

It's surprising how many of my clients define themselves as incredibly successful, yet they aren't satisfied or happy. When we dig deep into how they define success, we often learn they're measuring their achievements by someone else's standards.

I first met Amy at a networking event. She was poised and thoughtful, and I was impressed by how easily she explained the need for and benefits of her start-up's software. So, I was a little surprised when, at the end of the meeting, she asked if I could take her on as a coaching client.

During our first session, she burst into tears, telling me she was terribly unhappy and didn't know what to do about it. She had put her life savings into the start-up, and she was the face of the company. She'd been working toward this goal for years and was mortified that it was no longer what she wanted. Her identity was tied to it, and on top of that, her family had invested in the company. For all these reasons, she felt obligated to keep the business going. She felt that leaving the company would be an enormous mistake — and it would mean that *she* was a failure.

During our coaching sessions, we spent a fair amount of time discussing her personal (over)expectations, values, and boundaries. Then, we spent even more time talking about who she was if she wasn't part of the start-up. By the time we finished working together, she had successfully exited the company, sold her house, and moved back to her hometown to be closer to her parents and family.

She found a steady job that gave her the sense of security she had been craving, and living near her family gave her a connection she had been missing. By moving away from Baltimore, she came to realize that the city was simply a stop on her journey. Going home didn't mean she was going backward, and leaving something that wasn't making her happy wasn't a failure.

After that move, Amy continued to reflect and challenge her beliefs. She realized that she really wanted to live abroad for part of each year. We started working together again to help her define what that would look like and what it would take for her to make the leap. As of the writing of this book, she has found a new role that speaks to her, meets her needs from a career perspective, and allows her the freedom to live her life on her terms. She plans to spend several months working remotely in Italy.

WHY THIS MATTERS

If you're measuring success by someone else's standards, it's not surprising that you don't feel truly successful or content. At some point, you have to make decisions based on what *you* want and how *you* define success, which means being a little fearless. This means having conviction — holding strong in your beliefs rather than subscribing to social norms or worrying about what others will think of you. Having this type of conviction takes courage and practice, but it's something that gets easier with practice.

Amy was living someone else's definition of success. Prior to considering what truly made her happy and how she personally defined success, even she would have said she was successful! She owned a house by the time she was twenty-eight, worked as a director at a health plan prior to launching her start-up, made good money, and had a lot of savings in her 401K. Successful, right? Who would want to walk away from that trajectory?

But despite all these accomplishments, things didn't feel right. It turns out Amy was living her parents' definition of success. Or America's definition. Not her own. I'm willing to bet you're doing the same thing.

This is where One Foot In, One Foot Out starts to rear its head. Before you begin to move your back foot off that dock and into the boat, you need to understand whose definition of success matters to you: Theirs or yours?

Definition of Success

What is the definition of success? *Merriam-Webster* defines it as "the act of succeeding," which always makes me laugh when they use another form of the word in the definition. But I digress. It then says: "a favorable or desired outcome; *also*: the attainment of wealth, favor, or eminence."[22]

Interesting, right? The dictionary assumes success to be the attainment of wealth.

Let's take that one step further. What is the definition of the American Dream? Encyclopedia Britannica (Remember encyclopedias? They still exist online!) quotes James Truslow Adams, who first coined the term. He says the American Dream is:

> "... not a dream of motor cars and high wages merely, but a dream of a social order in which each man and each woman shall be able to attain to the fullest stature of which they are innately capable, and be recognized by others for what they are, regardless of the fortuitous circumstances of birth or position."[23]

The part that jumps out at me in the entry is this: "... each man and each woman shall be able to attain the fullest stature of which they are innately capable, and be recognized by others..." To me, this explains why the concept of "bigger, better, faster, more" is ingrained in our society.

You were probably taught at an early age that you need to live to your fullest potential; otherwise, you are lazy, not motivated, and apathetic. In most cases, the fullest potential was probably associated with titles, job performance, and financial gains.

No matter what role you play in corporate America, you are constantly bombarded with messages about "growing the business" and measuring success by the revenue of the company. Capitalism instills this thinking into our culture, and the American Dream assumes you will be a willing participant in this venture.

But in reality, your fullest potential as a human is very different than your fullest potential as an employee, leader, or business owner. In fact, your definition of success is likely to be very different than the one defined above.

A Cultural Shift

In recent years, there seems to be a shift in how Americans view success. A 2023 study completed by the think tank Populace measures Americans' *personal* definitions of success against their *perceived* definition of success.[24] The top findings were as follows:

Success is about a meaningful life, not getting rich.

- Half of Americans' top ten priorities for success are about a meaningful life, including being able to do work that has a positive impact on other people, enjoying their work, being enjoyable to be around, having a purpose in life, and being actively involved in their community.
- Interestingly, being rich is ranked in the bottom third of all priorities (45 of 61).
- Most notably, Americans believe that *other people* would rank being rich as the single most important priority of all.

The American Dream is personal, not financial.

- Most Americans believe the American Dream is about personal success (the ability to achieve success on the things that matter most to you).
- But they think most *other people* would define it in purely economic terms (the ability to achieve financial prosperity through hard work).

Let that sink in for a minute. **The American Dream that we were sold when growing up no longer defines how many people view success.**

But the study shows a disconnect. While we may personally believe success is defined as having a meaningful life, we also believe that others think money and achievement define success. Therefore, we think we should strive for those things, too. The challenge? Most people don't believe this is how success should be defined. So why are we stuck in this narrative?

I believe a couple of factors influenced this shift.

- **Generational shift:** As baby boomers leave the workforce, it's driving a change. Baby boomers, born between 1946 and 1964, were strongly influenced by the idea of the American Dream. They identify as workaholics, overwhelmingly tie their personal value to their jobs, and measure success by titles and money.

  In contrast, Generation X, born between 1965 and 1980, values working smarter over working harder. They see work as a contract.

- **COVID-19:** In 2020, COVID-19 had a major impact on this shift and how we define success. COVID-19 gave us all a collective moment to slow down long enough to see what we were missing and view our lives differently. From flexible hours to remote work, it redefined the workplace and gave us an opportunity to see things differently.

As you can see, there has been a shift in how we define success, and it's time you understood what the shift means for you. You no longer need to be tied to the notion that money and prestige equal success.

What would be possible if you no longer believed success was defined by money and prestige? What would success look like for you?

My job is not to tell you that you need to be pushing for more. My job is to help you figure out your own personal definition of success and then help you achieve that.

To further illustrate this point, I like to share this fable with my clients.

The Fisherman's Fable

A businessman is on vacation in a small coastal village. Every morning, he watches a fisherman return from the sea with a small catch of fish. One day, he decides to strike up a conversation.

The businessman says, "Why don't you stay out longer and catch more fish?"

The fisherman replies, "This is enough to support my family and a little extra to share with friends."

The businessman presses, "But if you catch more fish, you could sell them and save up for a bigger boat."

The fisherman asks, "Why would I do that?"

The businessman, now excited, says, "With a bigger boat, you could catch even more fish, hire a crew, and eventually build a fishing empire! Then you could move to a big city, manage operations, and make millions."

The fisherman pauses and asks, "What would I do with all that?"

The businessman replies, "You could retire early, move to a quiet village, spend time with your family, and fish whenever you want."

The fisherman smiles and says, "But that's what I'm already doing."

WHAT YOU CAN DO

What if your definition of success is to live within your core values every day? What if your top success priority is to live a meaningful life where you're able to do work that has a positive impact on other people? What would change for you?

Define Your Own Success

It's time to open yourself up to the possibility that you're living someone else's dream — your parent's dream, your family's dream, or even society's dream. If you find yourself asking, "What will my family say?" there's a good chance you're living their dream and not your own.

The ties that bind us to who we are now are often based on external expectations of who we are supposed to be — the breadwinner, the doting mother, or even the doctor, lawyer, or family business owner. We inadvertently put ourselves in boxes and hold ourselves there for others and, to be honest, for ourselves. When we know how to get an "A" in a role, we stick with it.

It's time to take a look at the box you've put yourself in and decide if it's where you still want to be. It's time to stop seeking external validation to define your own success and begin seeing what is possible if you allow your true light to shine through.

The first step in breaking this cycle is to look at how you currently define success.

Most of us have never truly identified what our definition of success is. It's just something that sort of sits with us as a beacon. Interestingly, this individual vision of success is also something most people feel they never achieve.

So, do yourself this favor and write down what you think your current definition of success is. If you say, "I'll be happy when…" your definition of success is tied to that "when."

In my case, my original definition of success was related to title and achievement, but I continually moved the goalposts on myself, so I never achieved success (or reached my "when"). My current definition is about helping people (like you), living a life that feeds my soul, and being present for my family.

Your next step will be to redefine your own definition of success.

JOURNAL REFLECTIONS

Once you have come up with your current definition of success, it's time to reflect on it to understand where it came from and if it still fits. Then, you can finally create your new definition!

Reflect on your definition with these questions.

1. Where does your definition of success come from?

2. Does that definition still fit?

3. If not, what has changed for you? What matters to you now?

4. Write your NEW definition of success.

OPTIMISM IS YOUR FRIEND (SO IS ANGER)

It may seem like optimism and anger are opposites, but they actually work together perfectly. Optimism pulls you forward when things are tough, and anger will push you toward your goal when you need it the most. Harnessing both keeps fear and anxiety at bay and allows you to move through the One Foot In, One Foot Out phase and on to the Clearly Me! phase.

Two weeks before surgery, Ed and I talked with Elaina's teacher, the school nurse, and the guidance counselor. My surgery was happening during the school year, and we knew I would be in the hospital for at least a week. We were (obviously) not sure of the outcome. It was heart-wrenching to know I couldn't be there to help Elaina through whatever she was feeling, and we wanted the school to be fully aware so they could support her effectively.

After the meeting, the school nurse pulled me aside and said something I carry with me in all facets of my life to this day. She said, "I was a recovery nurse for thirty years before I came here. I can tell you with 100 percent certainty that the mindset you go into your surgery with will dictate how you come out of that surgery."

Until she said that to me, I hadn't realized the dread I was carrying within me. In one moment, I changed my mindset from fear and uncertainty to one of quick recovery and returning to my "normal" life. I began to look at the facts; I was healthy and young. I wasn't the person who was going to die on the table. These facts helped me rein in the spiraling dread I was feeling. I was going to prove I was stronger than this thing.

Immediately post-surgery, while I was still in the hospital, I couldn't wait for the next twelve hours to pass. Every twelve hours, something got better. I could swallow! I could turn my head without throwing up! I stood up (with *significant* help, but who cares!). For the first few weeks at home, this pattern continued — every twenty-four hours, something was slightly better. I took a shower! I slept for three hours straight! I went to the bathroom on my own!

As the weeks went on, my recovery slowed, and expecting a change every twelve or twenty-four hours was a lot to ask. But the optimism stayed. I walked one house further! The doctor approved me to drive! (Yikes, by the way. That should not have happened when it did.) And it was this optimism that kept me going all those months of recovery. That... and a little bit of well-placed anger.

As I learned to walk and then run again, I began to get angry. When I started running again, I would literally have to think left/right, left/right. Running, for me, is the place where thoughts go to prosper. It is the space my brain needs to filter thoughts, create ideas, and solve problems. And now, I was using every fiber of my being just to move my body forward one foot at a time. I had no room to think.

I was lost and *really* angry. How dare this brain tumor take running away from me. I wanted my running back. I wanted my life back! It was this anger that pushed me to work harder — go for longer walks, learn to turn my head while walking, and how to hold my line on the track again. This anger was specific, and it had a purpose. It drove me.

In 2016, I entered a local Fourth of July 5K race. Ed ran next to me the entire time, helping me hold my line, warning me when people were coming up on my left side, and making sure I didn't fall. At the awards ceremony, I was shocked to find I had won the Masters Division! When I accepted the award, I was crying. I turned to Ed and said, "Oh my god, I couldn't *walk* at this time last year. How did this happen?" When I think back, I realize it was the combination of optimism and well-placed anger that helped me win that race.

WHY THIS MATTERS

As you go through your own change journey, there will be a myriad of emotions. Some days, these feelings may overwhelm you. There will be times when emotions like fear, uncertainty, loneliness, or anxiety will draw you back to that dock where your social ties remind you of where you feel safe. But sometimes your emotions will pull you forward — to the boat.

This is where optimism and anger come in. One Foot In, One Foot Out is marked by this tension, this back and forth. It is normal to have feelings of fear and uncertainty. After all, you are embarking on a change that has caused you to look at almost every facet of your life and question whether it still fits. It's also normal to know with certainty that this change is what you want and to lean into it.

Benefits of Optimism

Psychologists and scientists will tell you there are many benefits to optimism — not the least of which is overall better health.

Optimists generally see challenges as opportunities and setbacks as temporary. They tend to have lower stress levels, better coping strategies, and more resilience than pessimists. Optimists are also more likely to continue working on a problem than pessimists. They typically have better problem-solving skills, more persistence, and higher achievement levels than pessimists.[25]

Additionally, numerous studies show that optimists have better health outcomes in general, including stronger immune responses,[26] better outcomes after illness or surgery,[27] lower risk of cardiovascular disease,[28] and increased longevity.[29] In these studies, health is accounted for, so the outcomes are all related to perspective. Optimists assume their future is the result of the work they put into it.

Now that you know what optimism is and what the health benefits are, your job is to find ways to tap into it more often.

Realistic Optimism

I am not suggesting you go through life relying on positive energy and ignoring your emotions. While positivity is an essential aspect of optimism, optimism is not unbridled positivity without reality.

I define optimism as "having a positive outlook on your future." *The Cambridge Dictionary* enhances this definition by saying it is "the quality of being full of hope and emphasizing the good parts of a situation, or a belief that something good will happen."[30]

My understanding of optimism is grounded in reality. Optimism isn't the blind belief that everything will be okay. It is founded on the belief that you can prepare and do the work to create change and then feel positive about your effort. It works within the confines of the world you are living in. It relies on your ability to *truly* understand your own reality while also choosing optimism. You research and prepare for change and then move forward with hope. That's what makes it so powerful.

Optimism allows you to quit your job without having another job *after* you've done the analysis to make sure you can still pay your bills. Optimism propels you to have a conversation with an important contact *after* you've done your research to make sure you understand how to approach the person.

The Power of Optimism

Optimism is the belief that what you're working toward will work out, not blind faith that something completely unlikely will happen. Optimism is fueled by the confidence and conviction that you've done the work to get to where you need to go. Optimism also helps reframe challenges in positive, approachable ways.

Seeing setbacks as opportunities: It will come as no surprise that I subscribe to the belief that, more often than not, a setback can become an opportunity. It may be hard to see, especially in the early stages, but optimism shows up as the simple act of looking at a situation and asking yourself, "What's the opportunity here?"

Finding the silver lining: Coined in 1634 by John Milton, the silver lining refers to the silvery edges of a cloud when it is backlit by the sun. There is literally light just beyond this darkness. Optimism shows up in you when you find that light.

Believing this isn't it: There's a reason there are amazing stories of people defying medical odds, people losing it all and coming back stronger, or people escaping horrible circumstances and going on to thrive. It's because deep down, these people believed, "This can't be it." They believed there was something better, deeper, more powerful for them to fight for. Optimism shows its heart when you need it most. It gives you strength when you realize that what you have is *not* what you want.

Fall down seven times, get up eight: This Japanese proverb is my personal mantra. Optimism is the courage to get up and start over. Optimism is knowing that even though the last try failed, the next one may not. Optimism is knowing that every try gets you one step closer to where you want to be.

Optimism shows up in many other ways as well. Your job is to start identifying how it shows up in you because you will need to draw on that optimism as you begin to step into the boat, knowing that what you're moving toward is better than where you've been. Your optimism will keep you going as you question who you are, who your friends will be, and what your family will say.

Tapping Into Anger

While optimism has its place, there's also a very real possibility that you're angry. In many cases, the change you're in the midst of dealing with wasn't your choice. When this happens, it is normal to get angry, especially if it's unfair. Inequity is one of our primal triggers, meaning we all have it. Inequity turns on the amygdala — our flight, fight, or freeze function — and always triggers the fight response. So, if you're being treated unfairly, it makes sense that your first reaction is to fight back, and it makes sense that you're angry.

The issue with anger is that it doesn't always help — especially when it paralyzes you completely, entices you to retaliate, or forces you to act like toddlers.

Anger is fueled by emotions of fear, hurt, and sadness. Anger is also the armor you've donned to protect yourself from feeling those feelings. To really process all of these emotions, you need to expel the angry energy to find what's underneath. It's only by pushing past the anger that you can start to understand the real issue and begin to identify what, specifically, needs to change.

I always work with my clients who are in the anger stage to get it all out. We yell. We cry. We say all the things we know we'll never say to anyone else. And if my client isn't done after our session, I give them homework to keep getting it out — on paper, crying or screaming in the shower, wherever they need to expel that useless anger. You will know you're done with this exercise when you feel so spent you could sleep for an entire day. At this point, you can see the other side of the situation and can feel the relief of letting go of the baggage.

When I was in the throes of my anger after surgery, I could barely function. I was mad at everything and everyone. I took it out on those closest to me, and at times, it became unbearable. Elaina and I even had to come up with a code so she could understand if I was mad at her or just mad in general. Thinking about that now breaks my heart. I went through the process above to define the specific things I was mad about — I had lost my coping mechanism, my happy place, my independence, and a bit of my identity. And I felt like they had been ripped from me without my consent. Until I came to terms with all of these losses, I couldn't let my anger go.

Once I defined these things specifically, I began to focus my energy on the things that would allow me to get them back. I ran next to someone and held on to them so I could practice turning my head and running at the same time, and then later, turning my head and saying the name of the thing in my eyesight (tree) out loud without falling. I began listening to music when I ran, so both my sympathetic and parasympathetic nervous systems began functioning together again. I ran on the track to learn how to run in a straight line. All of these things were purposefully focused on my recovery and ability to regain the specific things I had lost (my coping mechanism, my happy place, my independence, and my identity). My anger was now focused and purposeful.

There are things you may be angry about. Dig deep to understand what's beneath the anger, then use the anger to propel you to focus specifically on what you want to change.

WHAT YOU CAN DO

If you've made it this far in the book, you know there is something greater out there for you. This is optimism, and you clearly already have some in your system! But you may also feel angry about some things. This is totally normal, and you can use it to your advantage.

Increasing Optimism

Let's say you want to be more optimistic. How do you do it? Good news! Optimism can be learned, and it can be increased.

First and foremost, do not force it! Instead, take a look at your life and begin to recognize where optimism already lives. Maybe you have positive thoughts when you wake up in the morning, or you can innately see all sides of a situation. Find a space where optimism is already your friend, and begin to think about places in your life where you could add it. For example, how could you use optimism to address a challenge you're having right now?

Next, begin to notice pessimistic thoughts. "No one is going to like the new me." "I'll never find a job that can pay me the amount of money I need doing what I want to do." These are not only untrue, but they are also the pessimistic thoughts that will keep you on the dock.

And finally, find other people who think like you. Studies show that the people you hang out with impact your behavior. Here's a silly example, but it will help drive the point home. If you want to make a million dollars in your business, you need to hang out with other business owners who have million-dollar businesses. If you want to increase your optimism, hang out with people who are more optimistic than you.

Moving Toward the Boat

Right now, if you're reading along and doing the work, you are smack dab in the middle of uncertainty. Part of you knows you want to move forward and get in the boat. Part of you wonders why you're doing this. And another part of you is tired and just wants to step back on the dock and watch the boat leave without you. This is normal.

Optimism and anger are your friends here. Imagine the little engine that could, repeating, "I think I can, I think I can." You CAN. Refer back to the beliefs you defined earlier in the book (i.e., I must _____ in order to ____.) and think about how these beliefs hold you back.

Now, think about the possibilities. If those beliefs aren't true, what is possible? This is your optimism shining through! You picked this book up for a reason — you want to make a change in your life. You have the belief and conviction that something new and different is possible. That is optimism. Don't let it go.

Use your anger to focus your energies on the changes that will make the biggest difference in your outcome. Specific and well placed — that's how to use anger.

You can do this. Know that the questions will continue to come. That's okay. By believing the future will be better, you will propel yourself forward to step into that boat.

JOURNAL REFLECTIONS

As discussed, both optimism and anger can help you to get where you want to be. Optimism pulls you forward when you may want to give up, and anger can be useful in pushing you toward your goal when you need it the most.

The questions below will help you find your optimism and identify any anger you have right now. Think about these questions:

1. Where am I most optimistic in my life?

2. Where could I add optimism to my life?

3. What anger am I carrying around right now?

4. What fear and hurt lie below that anger?

5. How can I use that anger to my advantage?

YOU WILL FIND YOUR PEOPLE

Making these changes can sometimes feel lonely. It may feel like you're leaving behind everyone and everything you know. Don't worry. I promise you'll find your people, and they will love you for who you are.

Ed and I have been friends with Mark and Alice for over twenty years — before we got married and way before we had kids. Our relationship has ebbed and flowed in many ways. Initially, we were group friends — you know, when you hang out in a group but don't necessarily spend time together on a one-to-one basis. As we had kids, that relationship grew stronger, and we found ourselves in each other's lives on a daily basis. We ate dinner together at least once a week. They were on speed dial for all occasions, and we knew each other as well as friends do. I used to say they're as close as you get to being family without being family.

Mark was the first person I called when I was told I should resign from the Exchange, and Alice swooped in to make sure I was okay in the weeks following. He's also the same Mark who created a position on his leadership team so I could get back on my feet. When, on that fateful day in April, I viewed my brain scan, I told Mark that night — before I even told my parents.

A few months after my surgery, Mark was lucky enough to sell the business he had spent years building. It was a stressful time, and he and Alice were knee-deep in the daily ups and downs that come with selling a business. I was focused on recovering from surgery, realizing that things had changed and that I was never going to be the person I was before. Ultimately, I understood that I needed different things in my life.

As I began to step away from who I was, and they began to step toward their new lives, we drifted. I no longer fit into the world they loved. They often have parties. I can no longer drink the way I used to (I used to love my apple martinis!). I also don't like to be in crowds as much because I can't hear the conversations. Additionally, post-surgery, I began to lean into my naturally introverted personality without shame. Before, I would turn on my extrovert personality for parties, but I no longer felt like doing that.

The true separation took years — really painful years on my end. I felt like I was in middle school all over again. I didn't want to go to their Friday night gatherings. I was uncomfortable in the setting, and it was a constant reminder of who I wasn't anymore. But I didn't want to not be invited! Meanwhile, my anger was showing through. I was angry at the situation. But really, I was hurt, losing the people I relied on most in my life. I spent at least a year in therapy working through this to understand what was going on and define what the new me needed.

Ten years later, we have found a new spot in each other's lives. We are the "old friends" who get together at meaningful times — a dinner here and another old friend's birthday party there. I am finally comfortable with that.

All of us had a part to play in the separation. But if I really think about it, much of it was me, realizing that the new me was not fulfilled by what the old me used to love. And it wasn't until I realized exactly what I needed that I could let go of what was and focus on the new.

I am unapologetically an introvert these days. I am unapologetic about what I can and can't imbibe. I am unapologetically focused on individual conversations, and if you want my time and energy, I will give it to you — 100 percent. But please don't waste my time with small talk. The new me loves meeting for coffee, taking walks, and hearing your innermost thoughts.

I'm sad that Mark and Alice are no longer in our lives the way they were before, but I would also never want to have them change their ways to meet my new needs. I love them for who they are, envy their comfort in having so many people around them, and appreciate all of their friends who welcome us when we show up. I will always love them like family. At the same time, I love and respect who I am and what I bring to the table. And I know I don't need to jerry-rig myself into their world the way I tried to do for years post-surgery.

WHY THIS MATTERS

As you change, you will realize that some people who have been by your side may not be the ones you still need by your side moving forward. In fact, if you're making a big enough change, this is almost a guarantee. This will hurt. This will make you question your new path and make you wonder if you should just go back to who you were before.

Know this: You will find a new group that will love you for who you are now. And your former people will still love you — just in a different way.

As you go through Phase 3 with One Foot In, One Foot Out, hanging on to *your* Mark and Alice without allowing room for change will keep you from stepping into that boat. Truthfully, it's one of the main reasons my clients get stuck. Social ties are so important, and it's hard to recognize that relationships can evolve.

More importantly, you will find a place to land. Part of this phase is having the conviction that you will find your new people. The good news? Your new people are in the boat, waiting for you to join them. Once you define for yourself what the new you needs in a relationship, you will find your people.

Belonging

According to Abraham Maslow's Hierarchy of Needs, once the core physiological needs of food, water, and shelter are met, humans begin to need other things to survive. He has defined them in order of importance. After food, water, and shelter, the next most important thing is health and security, and right after that comes belonging.

So, assuming you can consistently feed yourself, have a secure and safe place to live, and are healthy, your next core human need is to belong. This is where family, friendships, and connections come in. The need to feel connected and belong is so strong that humans first seek to be loved. Absent that, admired. Absent that, feared. And absent that, hated. Think about your neighbor who complains about everything — there's a good chance this is their way of (subconsciously) connecting.

HIERARCHY OF NEEDS

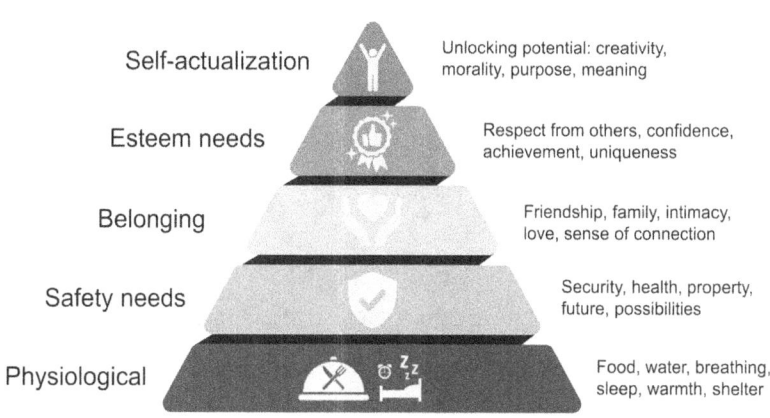

Maslow's Hierarchy of Needs. (Source: dlyastokiv - stock.adobe.com)

In the American Psychological Association's *Speaking of Psychology* podcast, Dr. Geoffrey Cohen, a professor of psychology and the James G. March professor of organizational studies in education and business at Stanford University, talks about the human need for socialization. He says, "As a social species, we are very attuned to whether or not we belong with our kin, and it's our fundamental concern about belonging to a group that drives us."[31]

He goes on to explain that the same regions in our brain associated with physical pain are activated when we feel socially ostracized, and our biggest trigger is not being seen. Cohen specifically talks about transitions and how, in the transition from one social world to the next, we experience belonging uncertainty, in which we subconsciously ask ourselves, "Do I belong here, and can I make it?"

So, it's no wonder one of the biggest questions I get asked is: "If I change, who will my friends be, and what will my family say?" During your journey, as you begin to recognize you want something different, it's normal to wonder these things. Your uncertainty about belonging is a normal part of any big transition.

Connecting With Peers

Studies have demonstrated that the people we surround ourselves with shape our habits, mindsets, and overall behaviors. You can call it peer pressure if you want, or the need to be seen, or the biological need to feel like you belong. However, study after study shows this to be true: Our behaviors are influenced by what we perceive as normal among our peers.

For example, one study found that people tend to conform to behaviors and attitudes around them to fit in.[32] Another found we are more motivated and likely to achieve our goals when we are surrounded by high-performing peers.[33] Yet another found that if your family or friends are overweight or obese, you have a 57 percent higher likelihood of being the same because of the social norms of diet and exercise.[34]

Surrounding yourself with people who see you for who you can be and who you are becoming will help you move forward. And, by the way, if you're worrying about what your current friends will say, it's a good indication that they may not be the right people for the new you.

WHAT YOU CAN DO

The most important thing you can do for yourself during this One Foot In, One Foot Out phase is to get clear with yourself about what you want. In this new world, what will be different? How will you be different? Take the time to truly envision what will make you happy in the future and what will be different about it from today. Taking time to set a clear objective for yourself and truly see your future makes it easier to communicate it to others and easier to have the conviction you need to keep moving forward.

It's also okay to share your new perspectives. The real friends in your current community will accept your new needs and allow the relationship to morph. For the others, mentally thank them for being in your life, recognize you have changed, and allow the relationship to take its course.

Fundamental Truths

I also want you to lean into some fundamental truths that will keep you looking forward and feeling optimistic, knowing you will find your new people. These are truths I have seen over and over in my coaching.

1. **Like energy attracts like energy.** As you begin to change, you will find others who think and act like you. They will be drawn to you just as you are drawn to them. You will realize it's happening when you're having a conversation, and you begin to hear the other person say things that you're thinking. Or, you realize you no

longer feel embarrassed by the things you're saying or hide what's really going through your mind. When these things happen, you have begun to build your new foundation. Pursue it! Find out where that person hangs out and see how you can join.

2. **You're most likely drained by some of your current people.** As you move through your change journey, you may find yourself not wanting to answer a text or not calling someone back. You may not be sure why, but I am. They no longer feed your soul. It's okay to let go of relationships that no longer feed you. It doesn't mean either of you has done anything wrong or that either of you is a bad person. It just means it's time to move on.

3. **Friends can come into your life for a reason, a season, or a lifetime.** If you think about it, you probably have work friends, family friends, neighborhood friends, lifelong friends, etc. Recognize which type of friend you have in a person and allow it to flow organically. You don't have to be all things to all people (neither do they, by the way!). You also don't have to be the same person your whole life. If things begin to shift, accept the relationship for what it was and let go.

4. **Loving yourself in a new way gives you the confidence to find a new group.** Being unapologetic about who you are and what you need allows you to step into a new situation confidently, knowing that you belong there! It's important to note that you may not find your group the

first place you look, but you *will* find it if you love yourself, know yourself, and believe in who you are.

5. **"I'm the type of person who..."** This is a remarkably
    powerful yet simple statement.[1] You can use it to shift
    your thinking as you define who you're going to be, the
    habits you want to build, and the change you want to
    make. If you want to start meditating, actually say, "I'm
    the type of person who meditates." This will open up
    your mind to see meditation as part of your identity. If
    you're having trouble figuring out who your new people
    are or where they hang out, try this on for size: I'm the
    type of person who... what? Then, find others who do
    the same.

If none of these fundamental truths help you, reground
yourself by reviewing your core values. Remind yourself *why*
these are your core values, why they drive you, and why they're
important. Then, refer to them when you need to figure out
where you belong. Others who have similar values will be your
new people.

---

1   This is a concept defined by James Clear in *Atomic Habits*, which is one
    of the best books out there. I recommend it to most of my clients. Clear
    does an amazing job of breaking down the psychological aspects of habit
    change. And let's face it, you're in the process of changing your habits.
    (So, after you're done reading this, read *Atomic Habits*.)

JOURNAL REFLECTIONS

Reviewing your friendships is an exercise that can sometimes be scary. Reviewing friendships is also an amazing way to identify where you could be tapping into the energy you need in your life. These questions will help you identify a person (or even the people!) you want to spend more time with and where a relationship may have run its course.

Take a look at your relationships.

1. Who energizes you?

2. Who drains you?

3. Who do you spend the most time with right now?

4. Who do you want to spend more time with?

5. Who do you want to spend less time with?

6. What does this tell you about what's important to you?

ONE FOOT IN, ONE FOOT OUT SUMMARY

You are unbelievably close, my friend. In Phase 3, you began to address the systems around you, looking at the social and cultural norms that have kept you in place until now. I know you have wondered more than once if you're making the right choice. And I know you still falter now and then. This is normal!

Your conviction is keeping you going. You've considered what success means to you. You learned how to tap into your optimism and parse your anger to make it work for you, and you've learned that it's normal to question who your friends will be after you make the changes you want to make.

At this point, fear is no longer pulling you backward. You are ready to step into that boat with conviction. With the work you've done so far, you now understand that it's okay to be the new you, and your passion for that new you will pull you forward.

When you started this book, you probably had an idea of what you were running from. Now, you should know who and what you're running toward.

You're running to the world where you leave behind the pieces that you don't want to carry anymore, where you are aligned with your core values and living within your new definition of success, and where your friends energize you rather than drain you. You are running toward a place where you're spending time on the things that are truly important to you, and you can embrace exactly who you want to be without embarrassment, fear, or shame.

The only thing left is to step off that dock and step into the boat.

JOURNAL REFLECTIONS

This is your chance to pull all the work from Phase 3 into one place. The questions below will help solidify how your new definition of success fits into your life and who your new people may be.

1. Who do you know who shares your definition of success?
   Note: You can usually see this through the values they exhibit and the actions they take.

2. What will you change now that you've identified your new definition of success?
   • What are you letting go of?
   • What and who are you embracing as you move forward?

Decision Point

THIS IS A MOMENT, NOT A PHASE

If you've made it this far in the book, you're planning to make a significant change in your life. Based on my experience coaching, this change will involve some sort of career shift — quitting your job, finding a new career, opening your own business, or retiring. It could involve moving to another state or even out of the country. In any case, it requires a decision and a commitment. You're ready.

MY DECISION POINT

About six months into my coaching business, I got a lucrative job offer to run a billion-dollar business for a stupid amount of money. I was elated. It was proof that I still had what it took, reminded me of the person I had been (and still loved in some ways), and alleviated all my financial fears of starting a coaching firm. Ed was *not* as elated.

"I can't see any reason we would do this other than greed," was his response. He loved having me around more, appreciated my being able to support Elaina, and never considered my identity to be associated with work. So, his perspective was quite different.

Remember, since I had been the breadwinner, losing my salary for the years it would take to build my business was an important discussion and the gravity of it weighed heavily on me every day.

What ensued was a very frank financial discussion about how much he made, how much we spent, and how we would make ends meet as I built my business. I told him that not only did he need to be okay with us dipping into our savings on a weekly basis, but that I needed us to invest in the business upfront. And he had to be okay with all of this without us changing our lifestyle. (I drove a hard bargain.)

He agreed.

I turned down the job.

This was my decision point.

YOUR DECISION POINT

You are still standing with one foot on the dock and one foot in the boat. You are emotionally ready to step into the boat. You have psyched yourself up. You have a lifelong friend standing next to you, telling you it's okay to step forward, and your new friend in the boat holding out their hand, ready to pull you aboard.

But the water is still choppy.

You wonder what to do. Will you make the leap? Or are you going to fall into the water?

As my daughter says, I got you.

The Decision Point is where dreams become a plan, where you begin to define the exact steps you will take to get across the water and safely into that boat. The Decision Point is driven by a hard look at your data and a reality check.

The Decision Point is about you looking closely at the reality you live in right now. So far, you have been focused on emotional changes. You have purposely not given heed to the financial, familial, or other real-life constraints that may be holding you back from truly stepping into the boat. The Decision Point is where you come to terms with these realities and decide to take action.

This is the moment you finally decide to take that step into the boat, the moment you push off the dock with your back foot, leave your body hovering over the water for just a moment, and actively step into that boat. This is the moment you decide you either are or you aren't all in. It is the moment your energy shifts. You're not running from something; you're running toward something. You're leaving your fears behind and letting passion be your guide. It is this conviction that leads you to the confidence to embrace the new you.

WHY THIS MATTERS

Change is an amazing concept. But it is just a concept until you create a plan to implement your vision in real life. Guess what? As your coach, I would never let you leave shore without creating that plan. This chapter is going to help you define your real-life needs so you can get in that boat and take off once and for all.

Finances and Reality

Throughout the book, we've been working toward a change that you want (one you've probably wanted for years). In the past, there's always been something holding you back from making the final decision. For many of my clients, financial concerns are the dream killer. For most people, the reality is this: either your change is going to impact your future financials, or your current financials are impacting your decision. Regardless, finances play a part.

Translation: It's time to look at your financials.

This is where we get real about what this change will mean. I am not the coach who simply says, "You can do it!" and walks away. I'm the coach who helps you see what is possible and then gets into the details with you to figure out what the changes you're talking about mean to your bottom line.

You cannot move forward until you define how the rubber is going to hit the road. This is the reality check that drives you to your decision point.

Financial Planners

We live in a world where it's easy to feel like we don't have enough money. We feel like we need to keep up with the Joneses, and we're told that we need to save for a rainy day. Meanwhile, we have no idea how leveraged the Joneses are, and no one tells us when it's okay to begin spending the money we saved. All we know is we need to *have* money, and we need to *save* money. For many people, these become shackles that keep you paralyzed.

I'm amazed by how many C-suite executives and business owners don't have a personal financial planner — someone who can look at their financial health with an objective eye. I say to my clients all the time, "Do me a favor; wait until *they* tell you to worry to actually worry about your finances. If they tell you to worry, *then* you can worry." Your financial planner will go into great detail with you about your long-term financial vision and then help you create a plan to get there.

If you don't currently have a financial planner, the most important thing you can do for yourself right this very second is get one. Put this book down and call someone you trust who has one they like, and then call that financial planner! Working with a financial planner is less expensive and more powerful than you realize.

If you can't find a financial planner through one of your networks, go to your bank. All banks have certified advisors who can help you look at your money. Don't pick this book back up until you've at least scheduled a call with a financial planner. Trust me.

In the meantime, while you're waiting for that meeting to happen, we will put some numbers on paper (or in Excel) to help you understand what your possibilities are.

Finance for Dummies

This is where you begin the process Ed and I went through to determine if my financial fears were warranted, because even though he had told me we were fine, I was still worried. Spoiler alert: In all the years I've been doing this, I have *never* seen a financial situation be as bad or as limiting as a client thinks it is.

Let's talk about how in-depth you need to be on your financials because I have found that looking at financials comes with lots of emotional associations that usually result in procrastination or, worse yet, all-out avoidance. For many people, *finances* are the thing keeping them from making their change. They fear that they need to keep making the money they're making now, or they think they can't afford to take the leap to start something new.

So, let's make this as simple as humanly possible.

Becca Math

We are going to look at how much you make, how much you spend, and how much you have in the bank that's relatively liquid. Ready?

1. Choose a time period that works for you based on your sources of information. For example, if you're a W-2 employee and get a bi-weekly or monthly paycheck, you can easily tell how much is going into your bank on a regular basis. Define for yourself how much you make in that given time period.
2. Now, we need to figure out what your expenses are. This can get complicated but just do your best.
   Usual expenses include:

   o Mortgage/rent
   o Car payment

o Transportation costs — gas, fares, etc.
o Utilities
o Groceries
o Cable/streaming/internet
o Entertainment – dinners out/movies/etc.
o School loans/school payments
o Charitable contributions

Make sure you're using the same time periods (yearly/monthly/weekly) and subtract these expenses from your income. The first step is that simple. The number you get shows what your savings should be per each defined time period.

3. Look at your bank account. How much money do you have sitting in the bank? Based on your expenses, do you have three months of liquidity? Six months? A year? Many of my clients are surprised to find they have more than they realized.

This simple math will ground you in the reality of your situation. If you're lucky, it will open your eyes to the fear you've been hiding behind, usually for years!

Finally, take this to your financial planner. Answer all of their questions, dream about your future, have them plug the numbers into their model, and see what comes out of it. I highly recommend you see what their model says in both your current state (how you're living now) and your future state (the future you've spent this book creating). See what's possible. I think you will be surprised.

Overcoming Financial Fears

Brenda has been a client of mine for years. For all the years we've worked together, her driving force has been money. More specifically, it's been her fear of not having enough money in retirement. This has been her primary focus. Even though her husband has told her for years that they are fine, she has never accepted that to be the case. She continues to be driven by the need to get to a certain number in her business — even though she doesn't *need* to, financially, and even though she's tired and ready to retire.

People fight very hard for their limitations, and financial worries are an easy limitation to hide behind. "Nope, I can't take that last scary step because I need the money." In Brenda's case, the real fear of who she will be after she sells her business is too scary to think about, so it's easier to hide behind the need for money to keep her right where she is. Money is tangible; people can't argue with you if you say you can't afford to make the change. So, the fear of money is a dream killer, and it's also often an excuse.

You have done all the work. You, my friend, are ready to make a change. And if your financials are telling you that you have room to walk away from what you've been doing and give yourself space and time to make your future a reality — do NOT look that gift horse in the mouth. This is the gift you have worked years to give to yourself: the financial cushion to make the change so you can live the life you've always wanted.

Defining Your New Income

Our next step is to get clear on what and how you will earn income in your new space. I have a client who left an executive director role to focus on a completely new career where she started from scratch. To make ends meet during her transition time, she did freelance jobs in her current career until her new career was lucrative enough to support her and her family.

How will you monetize your passion? What role are you looking for next? What is the expected timing of the transition? What can you do during the transition period to supplement your finances? These are all questions to be addressed during this analysis. (So, think about them now.)

Important note: This analysis is *not* meant to deter you from making the change. Don't let your fears take over during this process. This is to define a realistic path for you to focus on so you can achieve your change!

Create a spreadsheet for yourself with all of the above information (current income, current expenses, potential revenue streams). Project out where and when you think you will get future income and create a timeline for yourself. This process is the tool that will finally get you into that boat. By understanding your true financial needs and laying out a plan to sustain yourself, you are putting the power into your own hands.

Other Considerations

There are other realities that may be holding you back as well. For many of my clients, these realities often involve timing. For example, you may need to wait for your child to graduate. You may need to wait for the bonus to come through at work. You may want to finish a project before you go. You may feel like you need to hit a certain milestone.

Some of these are legit. Holding out for a thirty-thousand-dollar bonus for a few months may be the smartest thing you can do for yourself. And making a change when others in your family are also in transition can either be the right move or the wrong move, depending on your specific situation. But, delaying a change and using other external factors as excuses is *not* helpful, **especially** if you're harming your own health waiting for that external factor to happen. It's often hard to know on your own if you're making up the reason or if it's a legitimate reason to hold off on your change. Lean into a friend or coach to help you answer that question.

JOURNAL REFLECTIONS

Everyone has their own relationship with money, just like everyone has their own relationship with time. And all of us have preconceived notions about money. Often, this stems from our upbringing, but we sometimes don't give much thought as to why we have these particular ideas. The following questions will help you identify what is underlying your thoughts.

1. How would you describe your relationship with money?

2. What do you say to yourself about money inside your head? To help with this question, think about this: When someone talks about having enough money, what's the first thing that runs through your mind?

3. Where does this come from?

4. What did you learn about money from your parents?

5. How is your relationship with money impacting your decision to make your change?

DECISION POINT SUMMARY

You have done so much work. When you started this book, you knew you were unhappy, and you knew you wanted a change, but you weren't sure how to make it. You started by going through the Unfortunate Awareness phase, where you began to understand how you got to where you were. Then, you entered the Mourning the Past phase, where you came to terms with the fact that the old you and the new you could coexist.

In the One Foot In, One Foot Out phase, you battled the push and pull of your social ties until you redefined your idea of success and knew you wanted to make a change. But before you could be all in, you needed a thorough reality check.

The Decision Point reality check defines for you how much money you (really) need. It gets into the details of how long you need to stay where you currently are, how long you could go without the same income, and how to monetize your passion. It's amazing to me how often clients are pleasantly surprised by their own realities. They were sure they were going to be stuck, but the data shows them otherwise.

If you followed the steps I laid out, you have a high-level (Becca math) understanding of how much money you currently have as a cushion so you can pursue your new dreams. And if you followed my advice and have gotten a financial planner, you can work with them to create a future where all your dreams are a reality.

At this point, there is nothing holding you back. You have looked at your preconceived notions and redefined them; you have mourned the loss of the old you; you have addressed the social and cultural aspects potentially holding you back; and you have looked closely at the realities within which you live to help you see that this change you've so desperately wanted is truly, honestly, really a possibility.

This is your decision point. Are you in or out?

Either you are or are not
going to make this change.

Either you are or are not going to be the
new person you've worked to become.

This is YOUR decision point.

Are you in?

Clearly Me!

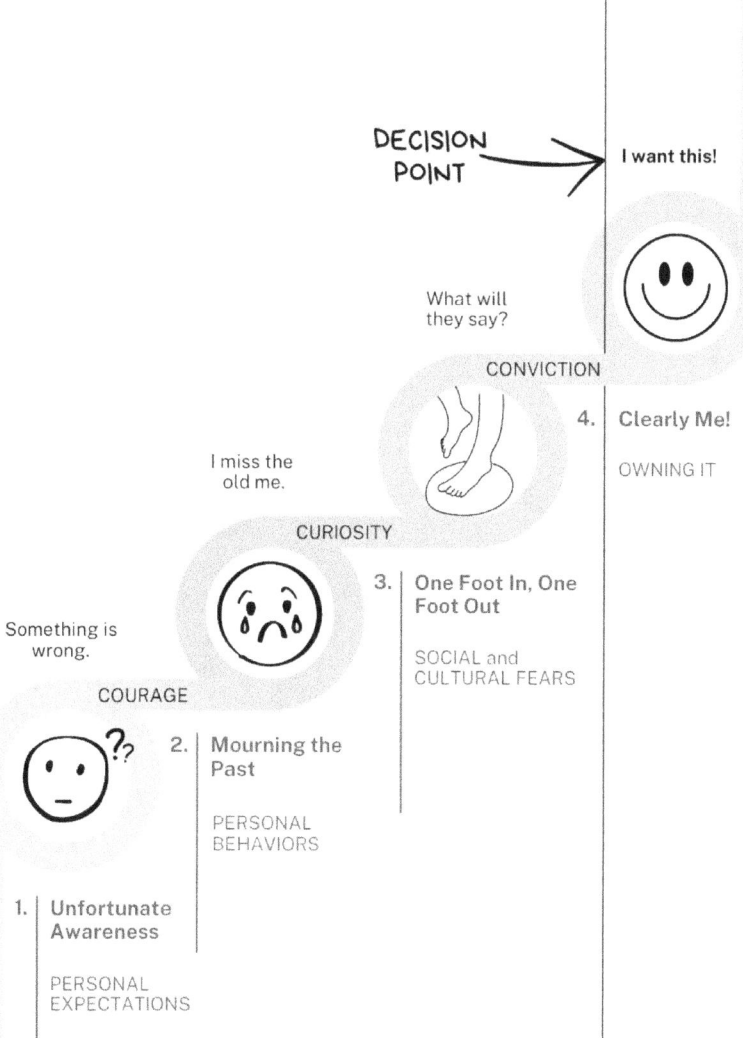

DECISION POINT → I want this!

CONFIDENCE

What will they say?

CONVICTION

4. | Clearly Me!

OWNING IT

I miss the old me.

CURIOSITY

3. | One Foot In, One Foot Out

SOCIAL and CULTURAL FEARS

Something is wrong.

COURAGE

2. | Mourning the Past

PERSONAL BEHAVIORS

1. | Unfortunate Awareness

PERSONAL EXPECTATIONS

CLEARLY ME!

You are IN the boat! You did it!

What You May Be Feeling

You feel amazing, right?

Not necessarily. If you're like my clients, you may be feeling like you could use some confidence. This is normal — and confusing. I mean, you've done all the work to let go of who you were and design who you want to be. You've worked through real-life constraints that could be holding you back. And that all feels great! Then why doesn't it feel the way you thought it would?

Realization

If that's how you're feeling, you're in the right place. There is a reason for a fourth phase of the process. The good news is this phase has only one mind-blowing realization — I Can Do This! I Want This!

This final realization builds on everything you've done so far. You've moved forward with courage, curiosity, and conviction. You can now step into your new world with confidence.

I CAN DO THIS!
I WANT THIS!

You've done the hard work and are ready to forge ahead. No regrets. It's time to embrace the new you, right? Yes, with one final step.

Even after I had committed to starting Extend Coaching & Consulting, I wavered. My insecurities and questions were still there: Was this really what I wanted to do? The further I got from my old career, the less relevant I felt. And what if I needed the income again? I was ignoring how hard Ed and I had worked over the years to create a nest egg big enough for me to take this step. And I was ignoring the gift of support Ed and those around me had given me. I wasn't sure how to move forward, and inside, I was still wavering.

I decided to talk to my coach about it. (Yes, I'm a coach with a coach.) I asked him why I kept wavering. He looked at me over Zoom and said, "Are you or aren't you a coach?" I was like, "Well, duh, yeah, I'm a coach." He said, "Then act like one. You either are or you aren't a coach. If you are, commit. If you're not, go back to health insurance."

That single conversation catapulted me into my business like never before. I stopped wanting the old me. I embraced the new me. I stopped hiding my new perspectives and shared them freely. I found my new people. I embraced the world of coaching and (metaphorically) began shouting it from the rooftops. I proudly told everyone who would listen that I was a coach, and I had opened my own business. I actively sought clients. I was no longer embarrassed about what I was doing or the change my career had taken.

Prior to that revelation, I was shy and a bit self-conscious about who I was as a coach and as a person. I had made a major shift from a hard-nosed executive who left her emotions at the door to a coach who purposely focuses on emotions to help people make scary decisions. It was a big change, and I was going through the process you're going through right now — wondering who my friends were going to be, wondering what my family would say, and wondering if I could make a living.

But after going through the entire change process, mourning who I was, straddling that water, and then finally doing the math and creating a plan for my future, I realized two things: I really wanted this, and more importantly, I could DO this!

WHY THIS MATTERS

This is the final phase in your journey toward the new you. It's the moment when you realize this is something you both

WANT to do and CAN do. Until you've reached this "want" and "can" moment, your dream remains an "almost" or a "could have been."

It's one thing to recognize and make internal emotional changes. It's another to assess your reality and decide that change is possible. And it's yet another to understand how much you WANT it, believe in your ability to do it, and confidently be this new version of yourself. This is your final step.

Words Matter

The language here is very important, so I want to spend some time talking about the relevance of "want" and "can" in this process. It's easy to gloss over the words we use, but I'm going to explain why we need to pay attention to them here.

Many people overlook the difference between the words "want" and "need" when they speak. There are important scientific factors that drive the value of "I want" and make it a much more powerful motivator than "I need." Let's follow the science.

Dopamine. When you *want* to do something, you activate the reward system in your brain.[35] Dopamine (also known as the happy hormone) is released, which makes you feel good. So, when you *want* to do something, the idea of the work needed to get there is backed by good feelings. Making you more likely to complete the activity.

Intrinsic motivation. When you decide you *want* to do something, you are using intrinsic rather than extrinsic motivation. Intrinsic motivation comes from within and is driven by your personal interests and enjoyment. Since it is self-driven, the activities align with your personal values, and the process itself is rewarding. (Refer back to the dopamine comments above.)

Intrinsic motivation leads to long-lasting and self-reinforcing change. It makes you care about both the outcome and the process, which increases your persistence and creativity. All of these factors reinforce your autonomy and sense of control.

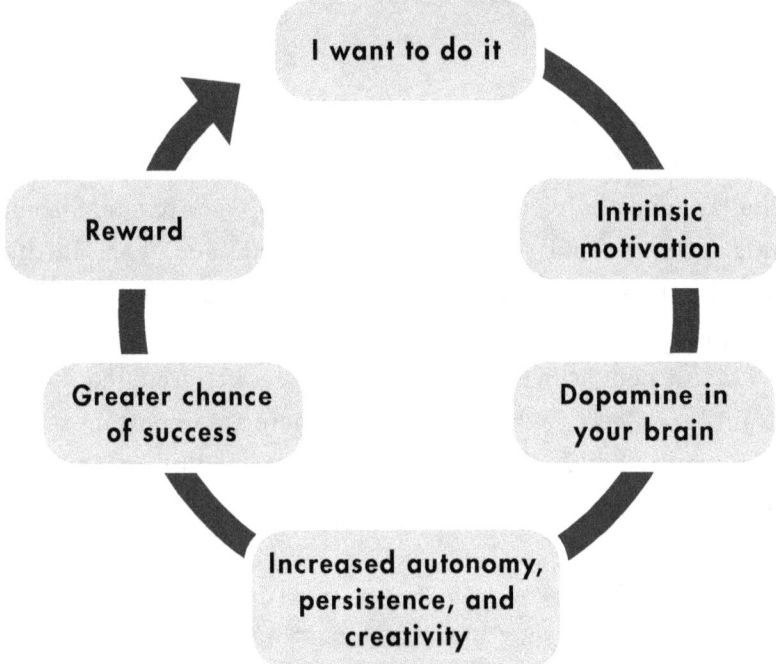

Meanwhile, "need" has different connotations. Saying you *need* to do something implies that you're not doing something the right way, not doing it enough, or are in some way falling short. "I need to" means you are subconsciously judging yourself, trying to force the issue.

I need to go to bed earlier. I need to work out. I need to call my friend. My question is this: Do you *want* to do those things?

Because if you begin to think about wanting to do them, you have found your intrinsic motivation.

If you don't want to do the things on your list but feel you need to, I can tell you there's an astronomically good chance that the thing you "just need to do" won't last a week because you haven't found your underlying want.

Think about a decision that was put upon you versus a change you decided to make on your own. For example, would you be more motivated to stop eating red meat if your doctor said you needed to because your cholesterol is too high or if you decided to stop because you don't really feel good when you eat it? In the first example, you are being forced to do something, and in the second, you are making a choice — you want to. Which feels better? Seems pretty simple when we look at it that way, right?

It gets a little murkier when the conversation is just in your brain. The words you use are very important. Your brain listens to them and acts accordingly by releasing the pre-defined hormone to do the job. For you to make this change a forever change, to feel the sense of control, to step into this with conviction, say out loud, "I WANT THIS!" and let your brain help you with the rest.

I Can Do It

Whether you think you can or you can't, you're right.
— HENRY FORD

Albert Bandura, a widely recognized cognitive scientist, introduced the idea of self-efficacy. Self-efficacy is a person's belief in their ability to complete a task or achieve a goal.[36]

In other words, self-efficacy is our knowledge that we *can* do it. Our own self-efficacy impacts how we think, how we act, and how we even see ourselves in the world. More importantly for you, it influences how we approach goals, tasks, and challenges.

If you have high self-efficacy (in other words, if you believe you can do something), there's a good chance you will. And if you think you can't, there's a good chance you won't. This is because, along the way, your mindset dictates your responses. If you think you can't, any setback will be seen as a huge failure. If you think you can, that same setback will be seen as an opportunity to learn, grow, and come out stronger. Additionally, if you think you can, your optimism increases and your emotions follow suit. You see how this all fits together.

| I want + I can | = | Optimism, Forward Focus, and Success |

WHAT YOU CAN DO

Not Sure You Want This Yet?

If you're in a place where you're still not sure if this is what you really want, we need to talk more. Remember, my job isn't to convince you this is the change you need (note that wording); my job is to help you clearly define the change you want (again, wording) and help you find a path to get there.

If you still aren't sure, try "I want…" on for size. Speak it out loud to yourself in the mirror. Tell yourself, "I want <insert change>." Now stop and feel. What is your gut reaction to this statement? How does it feel? There's scientific evidence that gut feelings are real. What is your gut telling you? Is this something you truly want? If so, it's time to revisit the steps in this book to understand what's holding you back.

If, like several of my clients, you know what you want to do differently but don't think you can do it because of your background or situation, look at the facts. Facts are key to taking your fears and emotions out of the equation.

- What has prepared you for what you want to do next?
- What transferable skills do you have?
- What do others say about your ability to do hard things?

Underneath "I can't" or "I don't think I can…" is the ugly truth of "I am choosing not to try." This is not you. I know you can do it. I know this because you've taken the time to read this book. I know this because my superpower is seeing in you what you can't see in yourself.

If you need help, find a coach who will get you over this very last hump. They can help you determine what you want and help you figure out how to make it a reality.

Let's Do This!

If you're with me, if you're sure you want this, and if you know you can do this, it's time to take action! Let's get tactical and make your dream a reality. Now is the time for you to create a plan to get you from where you are today to where you want to be tomorrow.

Throughout the process, you have identified and defined the things you want to change. Some of these changes can happen overnight, while others may take longer. Some of these changes depend on you alone, while others require others to change with you. All of the changes you make will require an action plan. You can use this plan to stay accountable and as a guide to continue moving forward.

Your Personal Strategic Plan

If you've spent time in corporate America, you've seen a strategic plan or two. You are now about to create your own personal strategic plan! Creating a personal strategic plan helps you clearly define your future and keeps all those details in one place: the work we've done together and any other thoughts or visions you may have. Get out your journal and put your plan on paper.

Change. Where should you begin? Start with the big picture. What is the overall change you're looking to make? Hint: It's the one you've been working on throughout this book. Define the change very clearly. Put it in writing, with specifics. For example, "I want to open my own executive coaching business within twelve months."

Realizations. From there, enter all of your realizations from this book. Add your core values and your new definition of success. Build your financials into the plan, so you know when you need to meet specific goals. Define your future clearly so you can review it regularly and ensure you're on the right track. Define what you're letting go of and what you're bringing into your life. Paint a clear picture of what your future looks like.

The Plan. When this is complete, you will have all of your thoughts in one place, and you have your plan. A picture will emerge for you of what you want to do and how you will achieve your change.

Set the Right Goals

There are tons of resources out there to help you set goals, so I am not going to get into detail on how to set goals here. I will, though, reinforce the importance of setting the *right* goals. The right goals are the baby steps you take to get to your overarching change. Without goals, you will not reach your vision. As they say, "Hope is not a strategy." If you're not used to setting goals, research SMART goals, find a process that works for you, and get setting!

Celebrate Wins

It can be hard to keep yourself motivated. After all, you have a lot of things working against you when you're changing! Your neural pathways, your own preconceptions, fear of the unknown, and fear of what your family and friends will say. All of these things can conspire to keep you where you are.

To keep yourself moving forward, celebrate the small wins. Doing so releases a short-term dopamine hit to your system, which gives you the energy to meet your long-term goals.

Find An Unbiased Partner to Support You Throughout

Every person in your life has a vested interest in your future, all the way down to your gym partner who needs you at the gym at five in the morning to keep them accountable. While most of them want the best for you (and I trust they do), *their* brains also want things to remain the same. Their neural pathways are used to the way you are in the relationship, and their neurons are lazy and don't want to change. Subconsciously, this can keep them from being unbiased in discussions with you.

To achieve long-lasting change, find an unbiased thought partner who can listen to everything you have to say without judgment and without a defined solution for you. Find someone who has been there before, gone through a significant change, and knows what it's like to do it. Create a contract with them to be your sounding board, hold you accountable, and ultimately, go through this journey with you.

I, of course, recommend a coach. The work you've done here is just the tip of the iceberg. You can achieve even more if you work with a coach. Find one who will tell you what you need to hear, not what you want to hear; someone who will help you find and stay focused on your long-term vision and will stand beside you and pick you up when you fall. There are many of us out there. Find the one that speaks to your soul. If *I* have spoken to you in this book, reach out to me!

EMBRACE THE NEW YOU!

Own this.

Live this.

Be unapologetic.

Wear the new you with pride.

You will know you've embraced the new you when you are unapologetic about who you are and what's important to you. When you wake up in the morning excited about what's next. When you're finally giving a voice to the thoughts that motivate you, and when you can honestly say you are happier, more grounded, more centered, and more aligned with your values.

When you get there, look back and congratulate yourself on your journey. You questioned your beliefs, chose what you wanted to keep, let go of the things that no longer served you, and embraced what could be. You are now a role model for others who are living vicariously through your strength, conviction, and the courage you had to change your life.

JOURNAL REFLECTIONS

It's time to look at your language to understand if there are any places where you still may be inadvertently holding yourself back. Use these prompts to explore this. Once you notice it, you can begin to change it!

1. When was the last time you said, "I need to"? What is it you need to do?

2. Do you *want* to do it? If you wanted to do it, what would that change?

3. When was the last time you said "I can't"? What is it you can't do? Is it really that you're just not willing to try? Be honest with yourself.

4. What if you *could* do it? What would that change for you?

CLEARLY ME! SUMMARY

When I first started coaching, people would ask, "Do you still do health insurance consulting?" I'd say, with confidence, "Yep! $350 an hour." And then they'd ask, "How much do you charge for coaching?" In a much smaller voice that ended as a question, I'd say, "I don't know. $100 an hour?"

Even though I was all in, and even though I knew I wanted it and could do it, it still took months (years!) for me to have the same confidence I had as the CEO of the Exchange. It was creating my plan, setting the right goals, celebrating small wins, and always having a coach by my side that enabled me to fully embrace this new me.

All of the work you've done throughout this book culminates in this final phase. Phase 4: Clearly Me! is the rest of your life. It is living in your new space and learning to build upon yourself every day. Phase 4 is believing in who you are and who you've become and then carrying yourself forward with confidence and grace.

You have looked at your language to understand where you can increase your optimism and forward motion. You've also begun to put together your personal strategic plan. With these tools, you can begin to live the rest of your life in this new space. Congratulations!

JOURNAL REFLECTIONS

As you put together your personal strategic plan, you may find yourself feeling a bit stuck thinking, Okay, it's on paper. What's next? The following questions will help you get over these humps. They are all forward-thinking prompts that will help you focus your next steps.

1. What will be true for you when you've implemented your plan and have realized the change you want?

2. What are the first few steps you want to take immediately?

3. What is the one thing (your North Star or guiding truth) that will keep you on track? Define it in a way so that you can reference it and check back in regularly. It may be one word. It may be an image. It may be a mantra.

THIS IS THE BEGINNING OF THE REST OF YOUR LIFE

Today, I got up to be with Elaina before she went to school, then worked for six hours before I took Nia for a walk. My parents are about to stop by to pick something up, and after that, I'm going to go for a run while the sun is still out.

Ten years after surgery and twelve years after the Exchange, I can confidently tell you that I am the happiest I have ever been. I live within my values, and my core needs are met on a daily basis. Extend Coaching & Consulting is thriving. I get to work with clients like you who know there's something better for them out there and are committed to looking in the mirror to make changes so they can live the life they want. I make time for my family and have hard boundaries on my time.

This past fall, I ran two half-marathons, placing second in my age group in a major race and winning my age group in a smaller race. I'm now faster (for my age) than I was before I had to learn to run all over again. This is possible because I found the time to regularly commit to something I wanted, did everything my coach asked me to do, and most importantly, believed in myself.

There are pieces of my life that I have gotten back through hard work, unwavering dedication, and a tenacity that won't let go. There are pieces of me that will never be again, through no fault of their own. And there are pieces of me that are new and improved, kinder and gentler, and less rough around the edges. I am unapologetic about who I am. I am proud of the work I've done to get to where I am and of the work my clients and I do together to help them make significant, powerful, and long-lasting changes.

I want to be clear about two things:

1. I am not ALWAYS this person. I am human, just like you. I lose sight of things now and then, worry about finances when I don't need to, and even dislike my business every once in a while. But I return to what I know is true to ground me. The truth is that I'm happy, and I know I'm on the right track.

2. Please don't confuse anything I've said in this book to translate to "I'm glad I had a brain tumor." I will never say that. The past ten years have been hard, and my continuing medical issues will be with me for the rest of my life. They may even shorten it in the long run. I am not happy I had a brain tumor. I am happy I used the opportunity to reevaluate my life and let go of the things that no longer suited me.

Along with some guts, planning, and strong people beside me, two things — taking the time to reevaluate and then letting go — enabled me to take a ninety-degree turn and find the happiness I was looking for. It was my ability to say, "Why did this happen? What am I going to do with this?" that got me to where I am now.

It hasn't been easy, and the line to get here has not been straight. But the realizations I share with you in this book are the ones that fundamentally changed the way I see the world. I am a different person than I was as the CEO of the Exchange, and I am a different person than I was prior to surgery. I now appreciate every moment I'm given in a new way. It's sixty degrees and raining in June? Thank goodness I'm alive!

Now it's your turn, my friend.

If you have done all the exercises in this book, you have:

- Defined your core beliefs, questioned them, and created new ones
- Assessed how you spend your time and become more intentional about how you will spend your time going forward
- Leaned into vulnerability
- Started to set boundaries around you and your job
- Redefined your core values
- Created your own definition of success
- Learned how to lean into optimism and when you should channel anger
- Gotten real by looking at your financial situation
- Embraced the change you want to make by knowing you want it and believing you can do it
- Created your own personal strategic plan to make your change a reality

Take what you've learned in this book, and don't let go. Dig deeper to find out more. Challenge yourself to take bigger risks. Dream big! Then, find a way to make those dreams a reality.

You've got this!

JOURNAL REFLECTIONS

As a final reflection, I want you to look at the big picture. How have you changed? Up until now, you have focused on small pieces of you. Reflect on these to allow yourself the space to see yourself differently.

1. Write about your experience with this book. What were the most eye-opening moments for you? What revelations will you carry with you moving forward?

2. How are you different now than you were when you started this book?

3. What change (or changes) will you make as a result of reading this book?

4. Who do you know who also needs to read this book?

THANK YOU

It took years for me to come to terms with the fact that there might be people who wanted to hear my story and who could benefit from what I have to say. Thank you to all of you who have said to me at some point, "You know, you should write a book," and to those of you who have said to me, "I changed my life because I heard your story and thought, if you can do it, I can do it." To all of you who played a part, thank you. It was you who brought this to life.

And thank you, reader, for believing in yourself enough to put my book in your hands and for believing in me enough to put yourself into my hands, if only for a moment.

It is an honor that you have chosen to spend your time with me.

ENDNOTES

1   Nikolopoulou, K. (2023) "False cause fallacy: Definition &
    examples," Scribbr. Available at: https://www.scribbr.com/
    fallacies/false-cause-fallacy/ (Accessed: 31 January 2025).

2   Wheelright, T. (2025) "Cell phone usage statistics:
    Mornings are for Notifications," Reviews.org. Available
    at: https://www.reviews.org/mobile/cell-phone-addiction/
    (Accessed: 31 January 2025).

3   Geuens, R. (2024) "What's the average time spent on social
    media each day?" (2024), SOAX. Available at: https://soax.
    com/research/time-spent-on-social-media (Accessed: 31
    January 2025).

4   L'Oreal Thompson Payton, "Americans Check Their
    Phones 144 Times a Day. Here's How to Cut Back,"
    Fortune, July 19, 2023, https://fortune.com/well/2023/07/19/
    how-to-cut-back-screen-time/.

5   "Cell phone addiction: Stats and signs" (2022) King
    University Online. Available at: https://online.king.edu/
    news/cell-phone-addiction/ (Accessed: 31 January 2025).

6   "Cell phone usage statistics: Mornings are for Notifications,"
    Reviews.org. Available at: https://www.reviews.org/mobile/
    cell-phone-addiction/ (Accessed: 31 January 2025).

7   Sanfilippo, M. (2024) "After-hours emails & weekend work may be hurting employees," *Business News Daily*. Edited by A. Uzialko. Available at: https://www.businessnewsdaily.com/9241-check-email-after-work.html (Accessed: 31 January 2025).

8   *Merriam-Webster.com Dictionary*, s.v. "vulnerability," accessed March 8, 2025, https://www.merriam-webster.com/dictionary/vulnerability.

9   Brené Brown, *Rising Strong: The Reckoning. The Rumble. The Revolution.* (New York: Spiegel & Grau, 2015).

10 "Why we define ourselves by our jobs," *BBC News*. Available at: https://www.bbc.com/worklife/article/20210409-why-we-define-ourselves-by-our-jobs (Accessed: 31 January 2025).

11 Westover, J.H. (2023) "The Dangers of Workplace Enmeshment: How a Career Can Consume Your Identity and What to Do About It," *HCI Consulting*. Available at: https://www.innovativehumancapital.com/article/the-dangers-of-workplace-enmeshment-how-a-career-can-consume-your-identity-and-what-to-do-about-it (Accessed: 31 January 2025).

12 Fryers, T. (2006) "Work, identity and health, Clinical practice and epidemiology in mental health," CP & EMH. Available at: https://pmc.ncbi.nlm.nih.gov/articles/PMC1501011/ (Accessed: 31 January 2025).

13 World Health Organization, "Long Working Hours Increasing Deaths from Heart Disease and Stroke: WHO, ILO," **WHO**, May 17, 2021, https://www.who.int/news/item/17-05-2021-long-working-hours-increasing-deaths-from-heart-disease-and-stroke-who-ilo.

14 Wooll, M. (2025) "How are personal values formed? Discover the joy of a life aligned," BetterUp. Available at: https://www.betterup.com/blog/how-are-personal-values-formed (Accessed: 31 January 2025).

15 Wooll, *How are personal values formed? Discover the joy of a life aligned, BetterUp.*

16 Jane Shore, "These 10 Peter Drucker Quotes May Change Your World," *NBC News*, September 16, 2014, accessed March 14, 2025, https://www.nbcnews.com/id/wbna56060818.

17 Roese, N. J., & Summerville, A. (2005). "What we regret most... and why." *Personality and Social Psychology Bulletin*, *31*(9), 1273-1285. https://doi.org/10.1177/0146167205274693.

18 Gilovich T, Medvec VH. "The temporal pattern to the experience of regret." *Personality and Social Psychology Bulletin*, 1994 Sep; 67(3):357-65. doi: 10.1037//0022-3514.67.3.357. PMID: 7965599.

19 Dascal, L. (2015) "12 Things People Regret the Most Before They Die" *Inc.com*. Available at: https://www.inc.com/lolly-daskal/12-things-people-regret-the-most-before-they-die.html (Accessed: 31 January 2025).

20 Pew Research Center, "Where Americans Find Meaning in Life," *Pew Research Center's Religion & Public Life Project*, November 20, 2018.

21 George E. Vaillant, *Triumphs of Experience: The Men of the Harvard Grant Study* (Cambridge, MA: Belknap Press of Harvard University Press, 2012).

22 Merriam-Webster.com Dictionary, s.v. "success," last modified March 3, 2025, https://www.merriam-webster.com/dictionary/success.

23 Jennifer Murtoff, "American Dream," *Encyclopaedia Britannica*, last modified January 24, 2025, https://www.britannica.com/topic/American-Dream.

24 Populace, "The Success Index: Misunderstanding the American Dream," Populace, accessed March 8, 2025, https://populace.org/research.

25 Scott, E. (2022) "The Differences Between Optimists and Pessimists," Verywell Mind. Available at: https://www.verywellmind.com/the-benefits-of-optimism-3144811#citation-1 (Accessed: 31 January 2025).

26 Pressman, S. D., & Cohen, S. (2005). "Positive affect and health." *Psychological Bulletin,* 131(6), 925–971.

27 Scheier, M. F., & Carver, C. S. (1992). "Effects of optimism on psychological and physical well-being: Theoretical overview and empirical update." *Cognitive Therapy and Research,* 16, 201-228.

28 Rozanski, A., Bavishi, C., Kubzansky, L. D., & Cohen, R. (2019). "Association of optimism with cardiovascular events and all-cause mortality: A systematic review and meta-analysis." *JAMA Network Open,* 2(9), e1912200.

29 Lee, L. O., James, P., Zevon, E. S., Kim, E. S., Trudel-Fitzgerald, C., Spiro, A., & Kubzansky, L. D. (2019). "Optimism is associated with exceptional longevity in 2 epidemiologic cohorts of men and women." *Proceedings of the National Academy of Sciences,* 116(37), 18357–18362.

30 Cambridge University Press, "Optimism," *Cambridge English Dictionary*, accessed March 8, 2025, https://dictionary.cambridge.org/us/dictionary/english/optimism.

31 Geoffrey L. Cohen, "How the Need to Belong Drives Human Behavior," *Speaking of Psychology* podcast, American Psychological Association, accessed

March 8, 2025, https://www.apa.org/news/podcasts/
speaking-of-psychology/human-behavior.

32 Cialdini, R. B., Reno, R. R., & Kallgren, C. A. (1990). "A
focus theory of normative conduct: Recycling the concept
of norms to reduce littering in public places." *Journal of
Personality and Social Psychology*, 58(6), 1015.

33 Mas, A., & Moretti, E. (2009). "Peers at work." *American
Economic Review*, 99(1), 112-145.

34 Christakis, N. A., & Fowler, J. H. (2007). "The spread
of obesity in a large social network over 32 years." *New
England Journal of Medicine*, 357(4), 370-379.

35 BrainFacts.org, "Motivation: Why You Do the
Things You Do," last modified August 28, 2018,
https://www.brainfacts.org/thinking-sens-
ing-and-behaving/learning-and-memory/2018/
motivation-why-you-do-the-things-you-do-082818.

36 Cherry, K. (2024) "How self-efficacy helps you achieve your
goals," *Verywell Mind*. Available at: https://www.verywell-
mind.com/what-is-self-efficacy-2795954 (Accessed: 31
January 2025).

ABOUT BECCA

Becca Pearce is living proof that you can be chewed up, spit out, and sucker punched, only to come back stronger and happier. Her journey has taught her the value of vulnerability, the importance of optimism, and the imperative to find the life you want to live now.

After a twenty-year career in health insurance, culminating in a role as the CEO of the state entity implementing the Affordable Care Act, a series of life-altering events knocked Becca off her feet, leading her to question her identity and rethink her purpose in life. She left the corporate world to start Extend Coaching & Consulting, a firm dedicated to helping successful leaders find their own personal meaning so they can live the life they dream about.

People who work directly with Becca make significant, long-lasting, and meaningful changes that make them happier, more fulfilled, more satisfied with their lives, and more successful, effective leaders. Becca's mission is to significantly impact the lives of the people she coaches and to touch 10,000 people with one nugget of information that changes the way they think.

Becca holds a cultural anthropology degree from Washington University in St. Louis and an MBA from the University of

Maryland Robert H. Smith School of Business. She is certified as both an executive coach and an exit planning advisor. Becca was named a 2019 Woman of Influence by *I95 Business* magazine and a Strathmore's Who's Who in 2023.

Becca is an avid runner and an unapologetic introvert. After a weekend run, you can find her either on her boat with her family or doing a jigsaw puzzle. She currently lives in Baltimore, Maryland, with her husband, Ed, daughter, Elaina, and constant companion and best work friend, Nia.

CONTACT

Email:	Info@ExtendCoach.com
Websites:	ExtendCoach.com or MoreBeccaPearce.com
LinkedIn:	linkedin.com/in/BeccaPearce

YOU'VE READ THE BOOK

AND DONE THE WORK,

BUT YOU'RE STILL NOT SURE...

You don't have to do it alone!

Together we can design the life you actually want to live and take action to make it real.

In our one-on-one coaching sessions, we will:

Get crystal clear on what change you truly want

Identify where you are in the change model

Discover what and who you need to support your journey

Map your next bold, practical steps

www.MoreBeccaPearce.com

NEED A SPEAKER
WHO SPARKS TRANSFORMATION?

BOOK BECCA PEARCE
FOR YOUR NEXT EVENT

Becca Pearce is a gifted speaker who inspires leaders and individuals to embrace their unique strengths and talents to create a lasting impact. Her calming presence, confident delivery, and unexpected candor ensure everyone in your audience will leave wanting more!

If you want a speaker who will challenge your audience to think bigger and walk away with at least one nugget that will change the way they think, you want Becca.

CONNECT WITH BECCA
www.LinkedIn.com/in/BeccaPearce
www.MoreBeccaPearce.com

www.ingramcontent.com/pod-product-compliance
Lightning Source LLC
Chambersburg PA
CBHW071730120626
46550CB00002B/455